Legitimacy B‹

This volume addresses the normative legitimacy of the international order, asking how we can make sense of legitimacy claims of increasingly diverse global governance institutions and practices and how their legitimacy relates to and differs from state legitimacy.

State legitimacy is a central concern of modern political thought but is inadequate when applied to institutions that differ from the state in type, level of governance, scope, and much else. We need a new, tailored approach to the legitimacy of institutions beyond the state, especially international and transnational institutions. Such an approach includes foundational questions: what does it mean for institutions to be legitimate that have radically different purposes, means, interests, capacities, constituents, and roles from states? And what standards do such institutions have to meet in order to count as legitimate? The contributions to this volume seek to advance the debate on these questions at both abstract and more concrete levels. They range from conceptual questions about the nature of legitimacy and international institutions, to rule of law, to the legitimacy of the UN Security Council, the International Criminal Court, and occupying military forces in the face of challenges specific to their nature and context. Together they demonstrate both the promise and challenges of theorizing legitimacy beyond the state.

The chapters in this book were originally published as a special issue of the journal *Critical Review of International Social and Political Philosophy*.

N. P. Adams is Assistant Professor of Philosophy at the University of Virginia, Charlottesville, USA.

Antoinette Scherz is Postdoctoral Research Fellow at PluriCourts at the University of Oslo, Norway.

Cord Schmelzle is a Postdoctoral Research Fellow and Principal Investigator at the Research Institute Social Cohesion at Goethe University Frankfurt, Germany.

Legitimacy Beyond the State
Normative and Conceptual Questions

Edited by
**N. P. Adams, Antoinette Scherz
and Cord Schmelzle**

LONDON AND NEW YORK

First published 2021
by Routledge
2 Park Square, Milton Park, Abingdon, Oxon, OX14 4RN

and by Routledge
52 Vanderbilt Avenue, New York, NY 10017

Routledge is an imprint of the Taylor & Francis Group, an informa business

Introduction, Chapters 1, 3–6 © 2021 Taylor & Francis

Chapter 2 © 2019 Eva Erman and Jonathan W. Kuyper. Originally published as Open Access.

With the exception of Chapter 2, no part of this book may be reprinted or reproduced or utilised in any form or by any electronic, mechanical, or other means, now known or hereafter invented, including photocopying and recording, or in any information storage or retrieval system, without permission in writing from the publishers. For details on the rights for Chapter 2, please see the chapter's Open Access footnote.

Trademark notice: Product or corporate names may be trademarks or registered trademarks, and are used only for identification and explanation without intent to infringe.

British Library Cataloguing-in-Publication Data
A catalogue record for this book is available from the British Library

ISBN13: 978-0-367-69497-5

Typeset in Myriad Pro
by codeMantra

Publisher's Note
The publisher accepts responsibility for any inconsistencies that may have arisen during the conversion of this book from journal articles to book chapters, namely the inclusion of journal terminology.

Disclaimer
Every effort has been made to contact copyright holders for their permission to reprint material in this book. The publishers would be grateful to hear from any copyright holder who is not here acknowledged and will undertake to rectify any errors or omissions in future editions of this book.

Contents

Citation Information		vi
Notes on Contributors		viii
	Introduction: Legitimacy beyond the state: institutional purposes and contextual constraints N. P. Adams, Antoinette Scherz and Cord Schmelzle	1
1	Legitimacy and institutional purpose N. P. Adams	12
2	Global democracy and feasibility Eva Erman and Jonathan W. Kuyper	31
3	The international rule of law Carmen E. Pavel	52
4	The arbitrary circumscription of the jurisdiction of the international criminal court Thomas Christiano	72
5	The UN Security Council, normative legitimacy and the challenge of specificity Antoinette Scherz and Alain Zysset	91
6	The legitimacy of occupation authority: beyond just war theory Cord Schmelzle	112
Index		135

Citation Information

The chapters in this book were originally published in the *Critical Review of International Social and Political Philosophy*, volume 23, issue 3 (2020). When citing this material, please use the original page numbering for each article, as follows:

Introduction
Legitimacy beyond the state: institutional purposes and contextual constraints
N. P. Adams, Antoinette Scherz and Cord Schmelzle
Critical Review of International Social and Political Philosophy, volume 23, issue 3 (2020) pp. 281–291

Chapter 1
Legitimacy and institutional purpose
N. P. Adams
Critical Review of International Social and Political Philosophy, volume 23, issue 3 (2020) pp. 292–310

Chapter 2
Global democracy and feasibility
Eva Erman and Jonathan W. Kuyper
Critical Review of International Social and Political Philosophy, volume 23, issue 3 (2020) pp. 311–331

Chapter 3
The international rule of law
Carmen E. Pavel
Critical Review of International Social and Political Philosophy, volume 23, issue 3 (2020) pp. 332–351

Chapter 4
The arbitrary circumscription of the jurisdiction of the international criminal court
Thomas Christiano
Critical Review of International Social and Political Philosophy, volume 23, issue 3 (2020) pp. 352–370

Chapter 5
The UN Security Council, normative legitimacy and the challenge of specificity
Antoinette Scherz and Alain Zysset
Critical Review of International Social and Political Philosophy, volume 23, issue 3 (2020) pp. 371–391

Chapter 6
The legitimacy of occupation authority: beyond just war theory
Cord Schmelzle
Critical Review of International Social and Political Philosophy, volume 23, issue 3 (2020) pp. 392–413

For any permission-related enquiries please visit:
http://www.tandfonline.com/page/help/permissions

Contributors

N. P. Adams is Assistant Professor of Philosophy at University of Virginia. Previously he was a Postdoctoral Fellow at McMaster University (2018–19), Hamilton, Canada and a Research Fellow with the Justitia Amplificata Centre for Advanced Studies at Goethe-Universität Frankfurt (2015–2018), Germany. Adams works in political philosophy and philosophy of law, focusing on issues of legitimacy, authority, and civil disobedience.

Thomas Christiano is Professor of Philosophy and Law at the University of Arizona, Tucson, USA, and Fellow of the Institute for Advanced Studies in Toulouse (IAST). He is a Co-editor of *Politics, Philosophy and Economics* (Sage). He has been a Fellow at the Princeton University Center for Human Values; All Souls College, Oxford; and the National Humanities Center.

Eva Erman is Professor in the Department of Political Science at Stockholm University, Sweden. She works in the field of political philosophy, with a special interest in democratic theory and methodology. Erman is the Founder and Editor-in-Chief of the journal *Ethics & Global Politics* (Routledge).

Jonathan W. Kuyper is Lecturer (Assistant Professor) at the Queen's University Belfast, UK. He works in the fields of political theory and international relations, often with a focus on democratic theory and practice.

Carmen E. Pavel is Senior Lecturer in International Politics in the Department of Political Economy at King's College London. She specializes in political philosophy and the history of political thought. Her interests include liberal theory and contemporary challenges to it, ethics and public policy, international justice and the authority of international institutions, and environmental ethics.

Antoinette Scherz is Postdoctoral Fellow at PluriCourts, University of Oslo, Norway. She has previously been a Research Fellow and Permanent Member of the Board of Directors at the Centre for Advanced Studies: 'Justitia Amplificata' at the Goethe University Frankfurt, a Research Fellow at the University of Zurich and held visiting and guest positions at Princeton University Center for Human Values and McGill University. She works in the field of political philosophy, with special interest in international political theory, legitimacy, democratic theory, the people, and autonomy.

Cord Schmelzle is a Postdoctoral Research Fellow and Principal Investigator at the Research Institute Social Cohesion at Goethe University Frankfurt, Germany. His work focuses on conceptual and normative questions of legitimacy and authority, political institutions, and the status of moral arguments in politics. His first book, *Politische Legitimität und zerfallene Staatlichkeit* (Campus 2015), won the best first book award of the German Political Science Association (DVPW).

Alain Zysset is Lecturer in Public Law at the School of Law at the University of Glasgow, UK. Prior to joining Glasgow, he held positions in Durham, Oslo (PluriCourts, 2016–2017), Florence (Max Weber Fellowship, 2015–2016), and Frankfurt am Main (Excellence Cluster Normative Orders, 2014–2015). Alain's areas of specialization include human rights law (in particular the ECHR), international criminal law (in particular crimes against humanity and genocide), and legal and political theory (in particular human rights theory, democratic theory, and criminal law theory).

INTRODUCTION

Legitimacy beyond the state: institutional purposes and contextual constraints

N. P. Adams, Antoinette Scherz and Cord Schmelzle

ABSTRACT
The essays collected in this special issue explore what legitimacy means for actors and institutions that do not function like traditional states but nevertheless wield significant power in the global realm. They are connected by the idea that the specific purposes of non-state actors and the contexts in which they operate shape what it means for them to be legitimate and so shape the standards of justification that they have to meet. In this introduction, we develop this guiding methodology further and show how the special issue's individual contributions apply it to their cases. In the first section, we provide a sketch of our purpose-dependent theory of legitimacy beyond the state. We then highlight two features of the institutional context beyond the state that set it apart from the domestic case: problems of feasibility and the structure of international law.

One of the central concerns of modern political philosophy and political theory has been the question of state legitimacy. The canon of modern political thinking evolved simultaneously with, and in large parts as a response to, the ascent of the nation-state as the most influential and foundational site of politics and human society. The question of when and under what conditions a state was legitimate had important implications, *inter alia*, for just war, resistance, and loyalty. What went mostly unquestioned in all this theorizing was the nature of legitimacy itself. According to the 'traditional view' (Copp, 1999, p. 10), legitimate states have the (claim-) right to rule and subjects of legitimate states have political obligation; illegitimate states lack the right to rule and subjects correlatively lack political obligation. Political theorists mostly argued about what *made* a state legitimate – consent, fair procedures, or its instrumental value – but not about what it *meant* for a state to be legitimate.

Especially over the last two decades, this focus has shifted in two ways. First, inspired by the conceptual tools of analytic jurisprudence (Hohfeld, 1919) and philosophical anarchists' doubts, many scholars moved away from the established debate regarding the justifiability of the state's rights and powers. They turned instead towards previously underexplored conceptual questions of what exactly these rights and powers (should) consist in and how re-conceptualizations of legitimacy would affect the justification of state authority (Applbaum, 2010; Copp, 1999; Edmundson, 1998; Ladenson, 1980, Morris, 1998; Reglitz, 2015; Schmelzle, 2015, ch. 1). The second shift in the debate over political legitimacy concerned the object of legitimacy assessments. In an increasingly globalized world, characterized by a huge variety of supranational actors and the fragmentation of political authority, many theorists moved their attention to the question of legitimacy beyond the state (Besson, 2010; Bohman, 2007; Buchanan, 2004, 2013; Buchanan & Keohane, 2006; Cohen & Sabel, 2006). Discourses concerning the legitimacy of various international institutions like the United Nations, regional treaty organizations, and international law more generally were increasingly common. Yet understanding their legitimacy in terms of the traditional view as a right to rule correlated to political obligation is challenging (Buchanan, 2010). These institutions do not rule in the ways that states rule and political obligation does not capture the relationship between individuals or states and international institutions. Even more radically, legitimacy discourses get applied to institutions that do not rule at all. For example, NGOs (Rubenstein, 2015) and transnational corporations (Karp, 2014) do not generally attempt to rule or exercise authority over outsiders. Still, due to their influence on global public society, the legitimacy of such institutions seems open to consideration.

So state-centred notions of legitimacy are insufficient when applied to institutions that differ from the state in type, level of governance, scope, and much else besides. As the traditional concept of legitimacy is put under increasing strain, strain on the normative standards follows. It is not obvious whether the democratic standards widely regarded as necessary for state legitimacy apply to institutions beyond the state (Christiano, 2012). This is especially true because international and transnational institutions still operate contemporaneously with states and so many of the fundamental political tasks that require democracy, like giving people equal say in shaping the rules of their societies, are left to states. What is needed, therefore, is an approach to legitimacy beyond the state that develops an understanding of legitimacy and accompanying standards of justification for the functions and purposes of non-state institutions and the contexts and constraints in which they operate. It is the aim of this special issue to make some initial steps towards developing such an approach. The following questions are at the heart of our project: What does it mean for institutions to be legitimate that have radically different purposes, means, interests, capacities, constituents, and roles from states? And what standards do such institutions have to meet in order to count as legitimate?

The contributions to this special issue seek to advance the debate on these questions at both abstract and more concrete levels. The first two contributions focus on the conceptual level and theorize elements of a general framework for theorizing legitimacy and the challenges of extending such a framework beyond the state. N. P. Adams focuses on the role of institutional purpose, showing how different features of an institution's purpose affect the stringency of the justificatory standards that the institution must meet. Adams also describes the various theoretical roles played by purpose when we are more concerned with describing the purpose of extant institutions in all their messiness than theorizing what purpose could serve a justificatory role, as in much of the discussions on state legitimacy. Eva Erman and Jonathan Kuyper propose an approach according to which there is no single, pre-theoretical feasibility constraint on normative principles relevant for legitimacy, instead arguing that feasibility plays distinct roles depending on the institution and debate in question. Erman and Kuyper especially focus on how feasibility constraints will vary according to two factors: the function of the normative principle in question and the coherence of feasibility with other normative commitments.

The remaining four contributions consider the legitimacy of specific international institutions and actors. Carmen Pavel considers the rule of law as a legitimating factor and argues that the rule of law in the international realm upholds a diverse set of values which includes, most importantly, state sovereignty. But Pavel argues that the value of sovereignty is ultimately entirely derivative of how it advances individual autonomy, which should influence the weight that the international rule of law attaches to both state's rights and human rights. Thomas Christiano considers the legitimacy of the International Criminal Court in light of objections that the court's jurisdiction is arbitrarily and unfairly circumscribed, especially as the world's most powerful states are outside its jurisdiction. The fact that such states have not consented to the treaty is not a panacea, argues Christiano, because there are limits to the role of state (non-)consent and because fairness is a core element to rule of law.

Antoinette Scherz and Alain Zysset consider the legitimacy of the UN Security Council as a balance of three features: purpose, competencies, and procedures. They argue that the Security Council can be understood as justifiably aiming at both the maintenance of world peace and at the promotion of human rights while the expansion of its competencies to law-making is not sufficiently supported by justifying procedures. Finally, Cord Schmelzle combines substantial conceptual reflection about the nature of institutional legitimacy with an analysis of the nature of occupying military forces. Whether we understand occupiers as having a fiduciary purpose – playing the role of government while domestic institutions are incapable of functioning – or a transformative purpose – restructuring the basic social order – matters greatly for what powers they could rightly claim and for what standards they must meet to gain such powers. Despite their different objects of assessment, these four studies share the methodological commitment to exploring the meaning and conditions of legitimacy as relative to the institutions' purposes and the contexts and constraints in which they operate.

In the remainder of this paper, we further articulate this methodology and show how the special issue's individual contributions advance the debate. We proceed in three sections. In the following section, we introduce the guiding methodological idea that institutional purposes determine the mode by which institutions are justified, the scope of their authority, and the normative advantages that they may claim (I). We then highlight two features of the institutional context beyond the state that arise throughout the special issue, are especially characteristic of that context: feasibility constraints (II) and international law (III).

Towards a purpose-dependent theory of legitimacy beyond the state

Perhaps the most important result of turning our attention beyond the state is the recognition that both what it means for an institution to be legitimate and the standards it must meet to be legitimate are contextual. In many ways, this is obvious, if implicit, in the literature on state legitimacy. Disagreements about the nature of the state and what purposes it can or must pursue shapes the disagreements between, for example, anarchists and statists or libertarians and liberals. The hard question for extending legitimacy to the huge variety of institutions beyond the state is understanding how more radical differences in context matter for the legitimacy of that institution. This also connects to the global justice debate and its recent move towards questions of what justice means within certain institutional regimes (e.g. Sangiovanni, 2008).

Against this background, one methodological question jumps to the forefront: whether each institution and each context requires an independent and bespoke theory of legitimacy or whether there is a general theory of institutional legitimacy that could be applied to all these different institutions, including the nation-state. We think there is such a general theory that revolves around institutional purpose (for previous work in this direction, see Adams, 2018; Buchanan, 2013; Erman, 2018; Rossi, 2012; Scherz, 2019; Schmelzle, 2015; in this issue see Adams, Scherz and Zysset, and Schmelzle). Focusing on purpose is especially apt if institutions are considered as purposive artefacts: humans organize the system of norms and roles that constitute institutions in order to pursue some end (Searle, 2010). Since such organization constitutes the concentration of power and risk and is used to pursue aims that would otherwise be unattainable by uncoordinated individual action, the question of how institutions can be justified arises immediately. This is the question of institutional legitimacy at its most general level. Purpose structures the institution's form – including the normative advantages or competencies it claims, the ways it relates to other institutions and agents, and the effects it aims to have – so purpose also structures what advantages a legitimate institution of that type would have and what standards it must meet to have them.

The question of institutional legitimacy can be productively theorized at this general level to some extent but an informed descriptive account of a particular institution is necessary for any complete theory of its legitimacy. Any plausible general theory of legitimacy could only give a template or starting point for theorizing the huge variety of institutions beyond (and within) the state. At base, this is because legitimacy is an importantly nonideal evaluation. The point of a legitimacy discourse is to coordinate our responses to an institution under conditions of disagreement and disappointment; legitimacy's normative role is about how we can move forward with the flawed institutions we have, not about which institutions would be ideal (Buchanan, 2013; Rawls, 2005). Thus, an adequate theory of legitimacy for a particular institution is always involved in the messy empirical details of what the institution actually does and how it fails, how it relates to other institutions in its particular historical, sociocultural context, and what we can reasonably expect from it. We already saw in the previous section how the details matter with respect to debates over institutional purpose, whether with respect to the UN Security Council (human rights or peace), occupying forces (fiduciary or transformative), or international rule of law (individual autonomy or state sovereignty).

One recurring theme when considering an institution's purpose is its deontic status. The case for the legitimacy of governance institutions in large part rests on the claim that they are uniquely necessary to achieve a morally mandatory aim. If an institution concentrates huge amounts of power, issues rules that it expects others to submit to, and uses coercion in order to secure conformity, it cannot be pursuing any merely permissible aim. The risks and harms intrinsic to such activities require justification by appeal to the necessity of those activities for a purpose that is not only important but required. Sometimes theorists make this explicit, but it is worth marking out as an issue of special concern. Many of the questions that theorists take to be fundamental to the issue of legitimacy per se are in fact a matter of specific kinds of institutions attempting to pursue a particular kind of purpose in a very particular way. Not all institutions use coercion, for example, but when they do it raises particular concerns for their legitimacy; institutions that exercise power by setting and applying rules might be particularly normatively demanding because they restrict the autonomy of those subject to the rules (Scherz, 2019). When we move to other kinds of institutions with other kinds of purposes that rely on other kinds of means to pursue their purpose, different questions of legitimacy arise.

Legitimacy beyond the state and the problem of feasibility

Taking seriously the idea of legitimacy as a normative discourse for coordinating our responses to institutions in non-ideal contexts leads us to the second main theme of the special issue: feasibility. A more ideal normative discourse, such as justice is often framed to be, may articulate ideals without concern for whether and how such ideals can be achieved from the starting point of our actual world. On our understanding, theories of legitimacy cannot be idealized in that sense. Instead, they aim to explain how we should respond to institutions in the actual flawed contexts that we find them. If an institution is pursuing some purpose but often fails to achieve that purpose, it may seem illegitimate. But if there is no feasible way to pursue that purpose other than through the fundamentally flawed institution we already possess, that institution may be legitimate because of the lack of feasible alternatives. On the other hand, the lack of feasible alternatives may not matter for legitimacy when considering an institution that undertakes a desirable but not required purpose.

Although the debate over non-ideal theory has increasingly taken up questions of feasibility, theorists are only now bringing such concerns to bear on questions of legitimacy. This is because discussions of feasibility are mostly about comparing alternatives, which in the case of the state has almost exclusively been about comparisons between the state and the state of nature. Since the justifying purposes of the state cannot feasibly be pursued without the sort of organization and institutionalization that constitutes exit from the state of nature, contra political anarchists, the question of feasibility is relevant but essentially settled. Moving beyond the state demonstrates the importance and complexity of feasibility comparisons for legitimacy. Given the background of states pursuing fundamental political purposes, there seem to be a wide variety of options for pursuing our other aims at the international level. This is clear in international law, which right now operates through a hodgepodge of treaties, organizational mandates, regional organizations, ratified state law, and much else. But there are many alternatives, running the gamut from a return to mostly disorganized international anarchy through the current muddled middle to the fully organized global state pushed by some cosmopolitans. In part, the question of whether the status quo is legitimate depends on our judgment of the feasibility of alternatives. This includes the normative assessment of how feasible an alternative must be before it would make sense to abandon the status quo (which has the great virtue of actually being in practice).

Although it is intuitive that feasibility matters for legitimacy, it also seems contextual: feasibility in different senses matters in different ways for legitimacy evaluations of different kinds of institutions. Feasibility concerns arise throughout the special issue, demonstrating the variety of roles that feasibility plays in connection to legitimacy. Most obviously and explicitly, Erman and Kuyper address fundamental questions such as what feasibility means, when feasibility is relevant to legitimacy, and what feasibility constraints should apply. Feasibility also comes up with respect to whether an institution is sufficiently fulfilling its purpose (Adams) and whether an institution should pursue certain reforms, including whether failure to pursue those reforms threatens its legitimacy (Scherz and Zysset, Christiano).

In our opinion, the main through line in these discussions is the great complexity of feasibility judgments in a multilevel system with different actors that restrict each other's options (e.g. governments, state constituencies, private actors, and international institutions). In the case of the ICC, for example, changing the court's jurisdiction seems feasible for particular powerful states, but not for the court itself or for the international community as a whole. To make a judgment about feasible options and their relation to the legitimacy of an institution, we have to ask not only about which options are feasible but whom they are feasible for and why those agents are the relevant agents for legitimacy. These problematics arise at the domestic level but are exacerbated at the international level by the lack of an overarching sovereign and so the presence of overlapping jurisdictions, the multiplication of actors and levels of action, and the even larger power asymmetries in the international system. Whilst it is important to criticise institutions that only enshrine and reinforce these inequalities, we hold the view that feasibility restrictions remain important for legitimacy judgements if they are supposed to establish how we should act toward certain institutions and which actors to criticise for their behaviour.

The relevance of international law for legitimacy

Legitimacy discourses beyond the state generally look 'up' from the state to institutions at the supranational level. But questions of legitimacy are also coherent when applied to institutions 'beneath' the state, at the domestic level. There are legitimate businesses, legitimate religions, and so on. However, there is an important theoretical reason why theorists rarely address the legitimacy of domestic institutions. We have a settled practice for coming to shared legitimacy judgments about such institutions: domestic law. One of the functions of domestic law is to regulate institutions within its jurisdiction and so when domestic law is legitimate, we mostly subsume judgments of the moral legitimacy of domestic institutions to their legality. The domestic law does what we want legitimacy discourses to do in general: coordinate our basic practical responses to institutions. The law determines which kinds of institutions get the social support and recognition of legality, and then as individuals we use various other judgments to choose which legal institutions we further support and participate in.

This is one of the reasons state legitimacy is such a hard question: we do not have the higher-order practice of domestic law to settle legitimacy questions in practice as we do for the institutions we encounter in our daily lives. But this is also why legitimacy for institutions above the state raises hard questions: we do not have settled law to determine legitimacy for us. Or do we? Here the question of international law enters and complicates matters, in large part because the legitimacy of international law itself is much in question. We can only reasonably rely on legality as a proxy for legitimacy under a legal regime that is itself legitimate. Under a clearly illegitimate state, the fact that the state allows or disallows a certain kind of institution is no good indicator of whether these institutions should have the right to operate. Further, whether for domestic institutions or states, working within a well-functioning system of law is not only a proxy for legitimacy, it directly enhances legitimacy (Buchanan, 2013). Working within a legal system shapes and constrains the exercise of institutional power, most clearly making it less arbitrary, generating different kinds of reasons and lessening justificatory burdens.

States and international institutions in our actual world operate in a context where there is a substantial amount of international law, so no legitimacy discourse of such institutions can avoid considering whether and how international law as it now operates affects their legitimacy. A fundamental question is whether international law is itself legitimate. This leads us back to the question of the institution's purpose, this time for international law itself. Possible purposes range from mere stability, to regulating expectations and promoting cooperation, to universally securing human rights and equality (Pavel). Our understanding of the purpose of international law is relevant for what it means for such law to be legitimate, the standards it must reach, how it needs to be institutionalised to be legitimate, how it would affect the legitimacy of the institutions it regulates, and the scope of its powers. A variety of standards of representation in the law-making process are plausible at the international level, including through both states and non-state actors or a combination (Besson & Martí, 2018). Democratic standards have also been demanded of international courts in light of their centrality to the application (and arguably also making of) law (von Bogdandy & Venzke, 2012).

Even if international law is legitimate, however, it is unclear whether such law plays the same role as domestic law and so whether we could rely on it to serve as a proxy for legitimacy discourse for international institutions of various sorts or for states. Perhaps ideal international law would serve this function but there may not be feasible alternatives that could perform this function any better, in which case our actual international law may be legitimate without performing the legitimacy-conferring function that domestic law does (because it achieves some other legitimating functions sufficiently well).

To sum up: international law must matter for the legitimacy of institutions beyond the state but complicates our discussions in three ways. First, international law requires its own theory of legitimacy, including what it means for international law to be legitimate and what standards it must meet. Second, whether international law would play the same legitimacy-enhancing and proxy role as domestic law is unclear. Third, we need to determine how international law as it currently exists matters for the legitimacy of institutions here and now, whether or not it is fully legitimate.

Conclusion

We close with some reflections about paths for future research that this special issue has clarified and opened. First, the international case makes the distinction between instrumentalist and proceduralist accounts of legitimacy even more stark. Do we need democratic procedures for legitimate institutions beyond the state, and to what extent does this depend on the purpose that a particular institution is pursuing? Second, the legitimacy of institutions beyond the state in our world today is still legitimacy of institutions in a world of states, and so in relation to states. Does the membership of non-democratic states endanger the legitimacy of an international institution or can it be legitimacy enhancing? Is state consent a requirement or only under certain conditions? Third, individual institutions are in part defined by their relationships to other institutions, including what purposes they pursue and what feasible options there are. To what extent does the legitimacy of one institution depend on the legitimacy of other institutions to which it relates? And how should the objects of legitimacy assessments best be delineated given these interdependencies? Is the fragmentation of the international system an advantage, perhaps allowing greater accountability, or a problem that must be solved with increased integration and perhaps constitutionalization? Finally, theorizing legitimacy beyond the state may have some lessons for state legitimacy. In particular, to what extent does state legitimacy depend on effective constraining institutions both above and below the level of the state or on the state's compliance with certain institutions beyond the state? And might theorizing the legitimacy of interdependent international institutions help us understand how, for example, the legitimacy of the judiciary depends on the legislature and vice versa at the domestic level? Theorizing legitimacy beyond the state is very much still in the early stages of development, yet we hope that its promise, and challenges, can be clearly seen.

Disclosure statement

No potential conflict of interest was reported by the authors.

ORCID

N. P. Adams http://orcid.org/0000-0001-8580-0872

References

Adams, N. P. (2018). Institutional legitimacy. *The Journal of Political Philosophy, 26*, 84–102.
Applbaum, A. I. (2010). Legitimacy without the duty to obey. *Philosophy & Public Affairs, 38*, 215–239.

Besson, S. (2010). Theorizing the sources of international law. In S. Besson & J. Tasioulas (Eds.), *The philosophy of international law* (pp. 163–185). Oxford: Oxford University Press.

Besson, S., & Martí, J. L. (2018). Legitimate actors of international law-making: Towards a theory of international democratic representation. *Jurisprudence, 9*, 504–540.

Bohman, J. (2007). *Democracy across borders: From Dêmos to Dêmoi*. Cambridge: MIT Press.

Buchanan, A. (2004). *Justice, legitimacy, and self-determination: Moral foundations for international law*. Oxford, NY: Oxford University Press.

Buchanan, A. (2010). The legitimacy of international law. In S. Besson & J. Tasioulas (Eds.), *The philosophy of international law* (pp. 79–96). Oxford: Oxford University Press.

Buchanan, A. (2013). *The heart of human rights*. Oxford: Oxford University Press.

Buchanan, A., & Keohane, R. O. (2006). The legitimacy of global governance institutions. *Ethics & International Affairs, 20*(4), 405–437.

Christiano, T. (2012). The legitimacy of international institutions. In A. Marmor (Ed.), *The Routledge companion to philosophy of law* (pp. 380–393). New York: Routledge.

Cohen, J., & Sabel, C. F. (2006). Global democracy. *New York University Journal of International Law and Politics, 37*, 763–797.

Copp, D. (1999). The idea of a legitimate state. *Philosophy & Public Affairs, 28*, 3–45.

Edmundson, W. A. (1998). Legitimate authority without political obligation. *Law and Philosophy, 17*, 43–60.

Erman, E. (2018). A function-sensitive approach to the political legitimacy of global governance. *British Journal of Political Science*, 1–24.

Hohfeld, W. N. (1919). *Fundamental legal conceptions as applied in judicial reasoning*. New Haven: Yale University Press.

Karp, D. J. (2014). *Responsibility for human rights: Transnational corporations in imperfect states*. Cambridge: Cambridge University Press.

Ladenson, R. (1980). In defense of a Hobbesian conception of law. *Philosophy & Public Affairs, 9*, 134–159.

Morris, C. W. (1998). *An essay on the modern state*. Cambridge: Cambridge University Press.

Rawls, J. (2005). *Political Liberalism*. exp. ed. New York: Columbia University Press.

Reglitz, M. (2015). Political legitimacy without a (claim-)right to rule. *Res publica, 21*, 291–307.

Rossi, E. (2012). Justice, legitimacy and (normative) authority for political realists. *Critical Review of International Social and Political Philosophy, 15*, 149–164.

Rubenstein, J. (2015). *Between samaritans and states: The political ethics of humanitarian INGOs*. Oxford: Oxford University Press.

Sangiovanni, A. (2008). Justice and the priority of politics to morality. *The Journal of Political Philosophy, 16*, 137–164.

Scherz, A. (2019). Tying the legitimacy of international institutions to their political power (Manuscript submitted for publication)

Schmelzle, C. (2015). *Politische Legitimität und zerfallene Staatlichkeit*. Frankfurt: Campus.

Searle, J. R. (2010). *Making the social world: The structure of human civilization*. Oxford: Oxford University Press.

von Bogdandy, A., & Venzke, I. (2012). In whose name? An investigation of international courts' public authority and its democratic justification. *European Journal of International Law, 23*(1), 7–41.

Legitimacy and institutional purpose

N. P. Adams

ABSTRACT
Institutions undertake a huge variety of constitutive purposes. One of the roles of legitimacy is to protect and promote an institution's pursuit of its purpose; state legitimacy is generally understood as the right to rule, for example. When considering legitimacy beyond the state, we have to take account of how differences in purposes change legitimacy. I focus in particular on how differences in purpose matter for the stringency of the standards that an institution must meet in order to be legitimate. An important characteristic of an institution's purpose is its deontic status, i.e. whether it is morally impermissible, merely permissible, or mandatory. Although this matters, it does so in some non-obvious ways; the mere fact of a morally impermissible purpose is not necessarily delegitimating, for example. I also consider the problem of conflicting, multiple, and contested institutional purposes, and the different theoretical roles for institutional purpose. Understanding how differences in purpose matter for an institution's legitimacy is one part of the broader project of theorizing institutional legitimacy in the many contexts beyond the traditional context of the state.

The purpose of the state matters a great deal for the debate over state legitimacy. The most basic conflicts between political anarchists, statists, and cosmopolitans, for example, often comes down to whether or not the state is actually necessary or sufficient for achieving some purpose. Within statism, Rawlsian political liberals reject any perfectionist aim, libertarians claim that the state can only undertake minimal functions, and so on. How we conceive of the purpose of the state matters for our understanding of the state's legitimacy at a fundamental level.

In this article I explore how institutional purpose matters for institutional legitimacy in general.[1] Most discussions of legitimacy consider a bundle of specified institutional features that characterizes a particular institution or institutional type (Collingwood & Logister, 2005; Sangiovanni, 2013). For example, the state's purpose is often considered alongside how it uses coercion and claims authority. Thus it is often difficult to see the role that purpose plays apart from other features of the institution. While complete theories of legitimacy eventually need to account for the bundle of features as an interdependent whole, it also helps to theorize the features independently of one another.

Such independent theorizing is especially important as we develop theories of legitimacy for new varieties of institutions, especially beyond the state. Having theorized the features independently, we will be able to see more clearly how they interact in unique combination. We will also be better able to investigate whether theories developed for particular institutions are applicable more broadly. For example, it is an open question whether democratic conceptions of state legitimacy are appropriate for institutions that differ drastically with respect to purpose, means, and other features. This is true of political institutions above the state, like the United Nations, the European Union, or institutions with more specific remits, like the World Trade Organization. Answering whether or to what extent democratic standards apply to such institutions requires us to investigate how particular features of institutions matter for legitimacy, both independently and in various combinations. My goal here is to show a number of complex ways that institutional purpose matters for legitimacy, although complete consideration of even this one feature is beyond the scope of this article.

Here is the plan. In the first section I sketch an account of institutions and institutional legitimacy, showing how general features of institutions establish a prima facie justificatory baseline. In the second section I consider how the deontic status of an institution's purpose matters for its legitimacy. In section three I complicate matters, considering how degree of achievement of purpose matters and distinguishing extant purpose from hypothetical justificatory purpose. In section four I raise a variety of problems for theorizing extant purpose. Finally, in a brief concluding section, I suggest a way forward with a more minimalist understanding of institutional legitimacy.

Institutions and legitimacy

In the sense I am concerned with, institutions primarily consist of two elements: norms that define various institutional roles or offices and individuals who accept the norms, thereby occupying roles (Miller, 2009, p. 25). By defining the roles in a coherent way, institutions are able to carry out their most basic function of coordinating individuals' actions.[2] While this broad definition might capture informal collections of norms, for example 'the institution of marriage,' my focus here is on more formalized cases. Formalization enables collections of individuals to act collectively and so raises the question of the standing to act collectively.

At its core institutional legitimacy constitutes a normative status or standing, which an illegitimate institution of that type lacks.[3] For example, state legitimacy is usually understood as the right to rule: legitimate states have the right to rule and illegitimate states do not. This standing correlates to a specific uptake on the part of others; the right to rule standardly correlates with a duty to obey. The right to rule cannot capture the legitimacy of all institutions because many do not rule at all. Regardless of the type of institution, though, a legitimate token of that type has a standing that illegitimate tokens do not.

The nature of this standing is tied to legitimacy's inherently practical role: it coordinates our collective responses to institutions in order to enable institutions to function (Adams, 2018; Buchanan, 2013). To call an institution legitimate is to ascribe it a standing that defines its relationship to various other individuals and groups in such a way as to protect its ability to exist and to function. To call an institution illegitimate is to deny that it has such a standing and so to deny it such protection.

For such an evaluation to be coherent, two conceptual preconditions must be met. First, there must be a coherent whole that can be evaluated and attributed a distinct normative standing qua collective actor. Second, that coherent whole must have a constitutive functioning that is protected. We must have a bearer of standing and a way to delimit its protections in a principled way. Institutional purpose contributes both to organizing a group of people into a coherent whole and to defining that group's constitutive functioning.

Purpose shapes and structures a collection of norms into a viable whole, capable of coordinating individuals. Any collection of norms is bound to have conflicts and tensions. There is an indeterminate number of ways that any conflict between norms could be resolved. Why should this office or role have these powers? Why should it relate to other roles in this way? Without a guide to resolve these tensions, the collection will be incoherent, incapable of coordinating people in an organized way. The guide is the institution's purpose.[4]

The constitutive functions of an institution are those functions without which it could not undertake its defining purpose. It is these functions that are the focus of the standing that legitimacy constitutes and so they are a useful criterion for individuating distinct institutional types.[5] Universities and businesses are distinct kinds of institutions primarily because of their distinct purpose and constitutive functions. A private home that becomes a museum memorializing its famous occupant becomes a new kind of institution because its purpose and constitutive functions change.[6]

Institutional purpose need not be something that is explicitly and intentionally held by all or even any members of the institution; instead it is an organizing principle that is required to make sense of any collection of norms as being bound together in such a way as to contribute to the constitution of an institution. This purpose can be very simple; at the limit, as explored below, an institution's purpose might simply be to share a set of norms. While institutional purpose can be merely implicit or very simple, it is more common for institutional purpose to be explicit and to aim at further goals.

Given that institutions are necessarily directed at and shaped by some purpose, the most basic normative question for any given institution is whether it is an appropriate tool for achieving the purpose in question. This question admits of various interpretations. We might ask whether the institution is the most efficient way to achieve some purpose. We might ask whether it is the only way to achieve some purpose – whether the state is the only way to achieve justice, for example, or whether membership in a particular church is the only way to get into right relationship with the divine. Among these interpretation, legitimacy asks: does this institution have the *right* to pursue its purpose? Must we collectively let this institution exist and undertake its constitutive functions, or not?

For an institution to be legitimate must mean that it has the right to exist qua means for pursuing its purpose or, as I call it, the right to function. As I understand it, the right to function is a claim-right against coercive interference in the constitutive functioning of the institution.[7] Coercively interfering in the constitutive functioning of an institution amounts to preventing it from pursuing its purpose and so renders it a non-viable token of its type. Legitimacy, regardless of whether we conceive of it as also including anything more robust such as a right to rule, must include the right to coordinate people towards achieving some purpose.

In order to inquire into the role of institutional purpose in a relatively ecumenical way, here I focus on the right to function as the core of legitimacy on any account. Focusing on the right to function allows us to ask the following general questions: under what conditions does a group of people have the right to accept a set of norms and coordinate their behavior in order to collectively pursue some purpose, such that others have a duty not to prevent them from so doing? How does the nature of that purpose matter for the conditions under which that right can be gained or lost?

Inquiring into these questions is the task of the rest of the article, informed by two important features of institutions in general. First, institutions produce a variety of goods by their very nature, including the goods of association, cooperation, and organization (Levy, 2015). Further, individuals' fundamental rights to self-determination include both the right to free association and the right to accept and bide by norms that structure our lives. An institution has a prima facie case for its right to function simply because it is a result of the free, protected choices of individuals and because it generates certain goods.[8]

The strength of this prima facie case is a matter of some contention that I do not address here but which matters a great deal for our final understanding of the legitimacy of a variety of institutions. One likely implication is worth noting because it also helps clarify the role of institutional purpose. There are many institutions that do not seem to have a purpose in the strong sense that, for example, we associate with institutions that have mission statements. A neighborhood's social club doesn't undertake any grand programs. But these institutions do have a purpose: organizing people. Regardless of whether they also pursue some further purpose, forming an institution allows them to gain the benefits of association and cooperation in a structured manner, reliably securing various goods. The goods of institutionalization can be the sole purpose of an institution. On my reading of the strength of the prima facie case for institutions' right to function, such limited institutions are legitimate ceteris paribus.

It is worth asking, though, why we should conceive of an institution as the result of voluntary choice, and so worthy of the protections we grant such choices.[9] Some institutions are the result of the voluntary associational choices of their members and some are not; membership in the state is most commonly not a voluntary act. Of course, when an institution is not voluntary in the right way, this raises immense questions for its legitimacy. The question I must address here is a methodological one: why take the voluntary institution as the default case, from which we construct our initial understanding of legitimacy? We might instead take involuntary membership in institutions, like the state or an ethnic group or often a religion, to be more fundamental.

In short, I think that it is much more difficult to make sense of legitimacy if we take involuntary membership as the base case. Being involuntarily obligated to join some group and to abide by its norms runs directly contrary to liberal egalitarian individualism, which is the general normative framework within which I am making my argument. Understanding legitimacy is difficult and nuanced enough in the case of voluntary institutions that adding the fundamental problem of nonvoluntariness seems to make the question profoundly difficult to answer. But ultimately I am a methodological pluralist and am happy to admit that every starting point, including my own, will illuminate some issues but obscure others.

In opposition to the prima face positive case for an institution's legitimacy arising from voluntary choice and freedom of association, there is a prima facie negative case because institutions constitute a concentration of power precisely because they gather and coordinate the efforts of many individuals. Choosing to concentrate any significant amount of power is prima facie unjustified for a variety of reasons. One is that concentrating power is risky and people have rights against unreasonable levels of risk. Another is that, at least according to some views, concentrating power is in itself a harm when it is not controlled, e.g. on views which construe freedom as non-domination and domination as arbitrary power (e.g. Pettit, 1997). So there is also a prima facie case against an institution's right to function because it generates certain risks or harms, some of which others may have rights against. The strength of this case largely depends on the type and magnitude of power in question and so on the size and nature of the institution. Small social clubs are legitimate ceteris paribus in part because they concentrate very little power. With these two baseline elements of the case for institutional legitimacy in hand, we turn to the role of purpose.

Deontic status

I noted at the outset that purpose is only one of the features of an institution that matters for an institution's legitimacy. Even narrowing my focus to only one feature, here I cannot explain all the ways in which purpose matters for legitimacy. For example, it is clear that purpose will shape how an institution functions and so what further claims and rights will follow from the more general right to function, yet I do not pursue this issue here.[10] Instead I focus on only one question: how purpose matters for the *stringency* of the standards that an institution must meet to be legitimate. I characterize this as how institutional purpose can raise or lower the justificatory bar for the right to function. Some purposes – or feature of that purpose – will raise the bar, i.e. an institution with that purpose must meet more stringent standards to have the right to function.

The standards for state legitimacy are more stringent than those for your local book club: the justificatory bar for the state's right to function is higher. The state has to separate out its powers, has to consult everyone within its ambit, must have limited terms for officials, must explain itself to its members, and so on. Your book club doesn't have to meet those same standards: it doesn't have to be democratic, or even formalized, in order to have the right not to be interfered with in pursuing its constitutive purpose. This is intuitively plausible. The question I address in this paper is how different institutional purposes matter in this kind of way.

Perhaps the most obvious evaluation we can make of an institution's purpose is in terms of its deontic status: is the purpose morally mandatory, merely morally permissible, or morally impermissible? The deontic status of an institution's purpose matters a great deal for its legitimacy. But we should not be too quick even at this early stage.

The first tempting thought is that an institution with a morally impermissible purpose is *ipso facto* illegitimate. This is too quick because of the prima facie case for legitimacy that institutions have in virtue of their members' rights to free association and self-determination more generally. This gives some weight to letting the institution exist – which is to say, letting members accept institutional norms and fulfill institutional roles. This might not be very much weight but it is enough to say that the simple fact of an impermissible purpose is not necessarily delegitimating.

Consider an anti-accountability club: a club that exists to coordinate people so that they can more efficiently violate oaths of sexual fidelity. Two facts about this social club seem to me to be true: (1) its purpose – more efficient breaking of oaths – is morally impermissible but (2) it has a right against coercive interference. This is related to the idea that breaking those oaths is impermissible but not the sort of wrong that others are justified in coercively preventing. The mere fact of impermissibility does not entail the absence of a right against interference.[11]

In the individual case, this amounts to the claim that people have the right to do wrong (Waldron, 1981). We have standing self-determination rights not to be interfered with which are not forfeit merely because we choose to act impermissibly. There are a range of impermissible acts that fall within our realm of self-determining choice that rights to non-interference protect. The same holds both of institutions qua products of our ongoing choices and of institutions qua collective actors. The right to do wrong has multiple grounds: the basic value of self-determination, the disvalue of (especially coercive) interference, the value of living together in a community of equals who all make mistakes and also all disagree, i.e. the demands of the burdens of judgment and pluralism, and so on.

All that said, the right to do wrong is limited in its scope. An institution like the anti-accountability club can be legitimate despite the fact that its purpose is impermissible because it is the sort of impermissible purpose that falls within the right to do wrong. But clearly many impermissible purposes fall outside the scope of the right to do wrong. For such institutions, our initial intuition is correct: merely having that purpose renders the institution illegitimate. Human trafficking is such a purpose; all institutions that have human trafficking as their purpose are necessarily illegitimate (the type is illegitimate). Articulating the principled difference between impermissible purposes that are automatically delegitimating and those that are not is an important task I cannot undertake here.

Moving away from impermissible purposes, a merely permissible institutional purpose is the standard case and in some ways the easiest to theorize on its own. The question is what other features of these institutions could override the prima facie case for non-interference grounded in morally permissible, rights-protected norm-acceptance and free association. For example, two institutions with the same purpose of financial gain might differ in their legitimacy because of the means they use to pursue that purpose: your local grocer uses fair market transactions for financial gain and so is legitimate ceteris paribus, while an extortion ring uses threats of egregious unjust harm for financial gain and so is illegitimate. Since our focus is on how institutional purpose matters for legitimacy, I leave these issues aside.

One general point before moving on: the prima facie case for the legitimacy of an institution with a permissible purpose has certain implications for what could delegitimate. If the prima facie case grounds a right to non-interference ceteris paribus, the question is how a right to non-interference can be forfeit. Rather than simply a balance of costs and benefits, the prima facie case shifts the justification into a deontological mode. I understand rights forfeiture to depend on culpable wrongdoing: an agent only forfeits a right she has if she violates others rights, making her liable to defensive, preventive, or punitive interference. So the mere fact that an institution with a permissible purpose is inefficient or produces some harms is not necessarily delegitimating. Only (sufficiently egregious) rights violations ground a case for illegitimacy.

The final possibility with respect to deontic status is that an institution's purpose is morally mandatory. This matters in at least two non-obvious ways. There are certainly more. In addition to the particular points I make, these arguments show that the role of institutional purpose is sufficiently complex to be worthy of independent and detailed treatment.

First, the normative bar for the legitimacy of an institution with a morally mandatory purpose is plausibly lower compared to an otherwise identical institution that undertakes a non-mandatory purpose. This may be surprising. It may seem that precisely because a morally mandatory purpose is so important, we should hold the institution that undertakes it to higher standards. But the idea that a morally mandatory purpose lowers the normative bar for justification becomes clear once we take seriously the idea that an institution is a tool that is by its nature risky.

For example, it is unjustifiable for Jane the ambulance driver to vastly exceed the speed limit just for fun, primarily because of the risks to bystanders. But it is justifiable for Jane to vastly exceed the speed limit when driving a seriously injured person to the hospital even if it involves the same level of risk to bystanders. Entertainment is a morally permissible goal but cannot justify vast speeds given the sorts of risks involved. With respect to the same risks, though, the mandatory purpose of rendering life-saving aid renders speeding justifiable.

I express this difference as a 'lowering' of the justificatory bar or burden on speeding. This is to capture the idea that a more demanding purpose can justify employing a greater range of means, including riskier means. When Jane is trying to save a life, Jane can justifiably impose greater risks on bystanders than she can for entertainment. Ceteris paribus, being obligated to act towards some aim means that a greater variety of costs, harms, and even wrongs can be risked than when merely voluntarily undertaking some aim. In general it is easier to justify risky activities to do more important things. (Parallel points hold for comparisons between morally mandatory purposes of different import.)

As argued above, the existence and operation of institutions is inherently risky because institutions concentrate power and thereby enable much more potentially impactful activities. A morally mandatory purpose can justify a riskier and even more harmful institution: an institution that is bigger, uses riskier means, and even violates rights sometimes. Consider criminal justice institutions, which we know will sometimes egregiously wrong people because sometimes innocent people are punished. These wrongs do not automatically render such institutions illegitimate. If they did, no human criminal justice institution could ever be legitimate because all such institutions are fallible. Yet the same fallible punitive institution is obviously illegitimate if it is set to purposes other than our most demanding and important ones.

This example brings us to the second point. A morally mandatory purpose makes the question of feasible institutional alternatives relevant (Pogge, 2008, pp. 25, 182). If there is a task that we are obligated to undertake and an institution is the only way to undertake it, then there is a very strong case for having an institution even if it is quite bad in certain respects. (This does not necessarily entail that when we are undertaking morally mandatory tasks, any institution no matter how bad would be legitimate if there was no feasible alternative. Sometimes the absence of any institution and so the failure to achieve the purpose is preferable, with reparative and ameliorative duties becoming the main focus.) But just because we need some institution to pursue a particular mandatory purpose does not mean any institution which pursues it is legitimate. Its legitimacy also depends on comparisons to feasible institutional alternatives.

Consider a morally mandatory task like providing medical care to sick people. Addressing health on an ad hoc basis is massively inefficient and very costly. To provide adequate care to the ill and health security for everyone regardless of current health status, we need institutions that train and employ medical professionals and are ready to treat people as necessary. Now compare the best, most well-funded medical institution in the United States from the mid-nineteenth century to a medical institution now; in particular consider the sorts of treatments that they make available and are competent to deploy. In the past, it was infeasible to have anything nearly as effective in treating illness as we have today, mostly because of a lack of medical knowledge and technical capacity.

The standards we hold our medical institutions to depend upon our capabilities because capabilities partly determine which institutional alternatives are feasible. In the nineteenth century there were no feasible alternatives to, for example, palliative care for cancer patients because we didn't understand cancer very well and had no knowably effective treatments. So a medical institution in the mid-nineteenth century that did not have any effective cancer treatments could very well be legitimate: it could have the right to carry out its tasks, to serve as a cooperative venture with the aim of providing medical care. If we transplant that medical institution, with all its capacities and equipment intact, to our time, it is illegitimate. The only thing that has changed is that there are now better feasible alternatives because we know much more and have much better technology. We should not let a medical institution with such poor treatments serve a contemporary community because we can (relatively easily) establish an alternative institution that serves the same mandatory purpose much better. When an institution undertakes a morally mandatory purpose, the importance of achieving that purpose can lower the justificatory bar such that the institution can be legitimate despite features that would render it illegitimate were there any feasible alternative institution for pursuing that purpose without the objectionable features. The presence or absence of alternatives can change whether it is legitimate.

On the other hand, when considering a merely morally permissible purpose, there is very little reason to have a harmful institution and so the presence or absence of feasible institutional alternatives is irrelevant to an institution's legitimacy. Whatever permissible purpose the institution was undertaking can by definition permissibly be abandoned since it was not obligatory. The features that make it objectionable render it illegitimate even when there are no feasible alternatives because the reasons to pursue its purpose at all are quite weak. Feasible institutional alternatives only matter for an institution's legitimacy when it is undertaking a morally mandatory purpose. The deontic status of an institution's purpose matters for legitimacy by setting the justificatory baseline or bar in a way that no other feature does.

Complications

In this section I uncover two complications and show how they need to be considered in order for us to more fully understand the role of institutional purpose for legitimacy. First, so far I have been relying on an ambiguity regarding what it means for an institution to undertake a specific purpose: whether we are considering cases where institutions actually achieve their purpose or cases where institutions merely attempt to achieve their purpose and may fail. This raises a variety of further complexities.

First, with respect to certain kinds of impermissible purposes, it may be that we only think institutions are legitimate when they mostly fail to achieve their purpose. Sometimes this is how we think of authoritarian or anarchist political parties in democracies.[12] So far as those parties fail to achieve any widespread support and do not threaten the democratic character of the polity, we think they should be allowed to carry on despite the fact it would be impermissible to bring about authoritarian governance or anarchy. The familiar reasons concern the value of free expression and association as well as the disvalue of concentrating and exercising power of certain kinds, especially with respect to suppressing political views. But it is also plausible to think that should such a party gain sufficiently widespread support and begin to achieve its purpose, it would be illegitimate and we would be justified in shutting it down with coercive force.

Second, with respect to merely permissible purposes, degree of achievement probably does not matter very much. Whether they succeed or fail may matter a great deal for the personal projects of the members, or even the community, but their failure does not render them illegitimate because it was up to them whether to undertake the purpose in the first place. Things are more complicated with respect to mandatory purposes.

The first thought is that failing at mandatory purposes is particularly bad – indeed, by definition wrongful – so institutions that fail to achieve a mandatory purpose are prima facie illegitimate. This ignores the fact, though, that some purposes are incredibly difficult or necessarily incomplete. I take justice to be a purpose with both features: it is almost impossible to do well and is a task that has no endpoint because even a just state of affairs needs to be sustained and protected intergenerationally, not to mention adaptive to changing contexts. If we think perfect – or even close – achievement of mandatory purposes is required for legitimacy, then any (human) institution with justice as its purpose will almost certainly be illegitimate. We need a more expansive and humanist understanding of legitimacy than that. Legitimacy is not an exercise in ideal theory.

This is not true of all mandatory purposes, some of which may have a determinate completion point that is relatively easy to achieve. For such purposes, failing to approximate the purpose or even simply failing to achieve it may render the institution illegitimate – again, assuming that there is some feasible institutional alternative that could do better (which is very likely given an easily achieved purpose). To return to a previous example, a contemporary medical institution that failed to mend broken bones or cure a common infection would be illegitimate because we know how to achieve these ends quite easily; a medical institution that failed to cure all kinds of cancer, on the other hand, can still be legitimate.

The second complication is about the role of purpose in justifying an institution and arises from questioning the standard strategy used in theorizing state legitimacy. Generally, questions of state legitimacy proceed from a description of the defining features of the actual extant institutions that we call states, especially including their relation to the basic structure, claims to authority, and widespread use of force. The question is then asked: how could an institution with these features actually be justified in some sense?[13] Theorists then argue that some *hypothetical* purpose could justify such an institution. This theorizing happens at the level of institutional type. The next step is to apply the theory to particular institutional tokens, arguing that states that do not undertake the justifying purpose or which undertake any other purpose are illegitimate.

This picture, even oversimplified in this manner, clearly only works in some cases.[14] It presumes a stable description of institutional features out of which we can construct an institutional type and to which the hypothetical purpose is then related. But such stability is not a feature of all institutions. In the case of the state, we have data for theorizing in this manner because there are hundreds of states and have been many similar but distinct institutional types over history. We have very few such resources in the case of many new international and transnational institutions, some of which are the sole token of their type.

Especially for rarer institutions that are not tokens of an entrenched type like the state, it may also be the case that they change their features dramatically over time, including their purpose. The European Union has become a robust, almost state-like institution but it began as a common market for specific goods. We could theorize the legitimacy of each time-slice of the institution but we should also concern ourselves with more liminal moments, especially because the EU is still affecting people's lives even in its liminality. The state's features are so worrying, and the purpose so demanding, that many possibilities for institutional change are in some ways normatively closed to us. When we consider institutions beyond the state, though, such change is a much more persistent feature that requires our attention.

In addition, we often want to work from purpose to other features rather than, as in the case of sociologically identified institutions like the state, from other features to purpose. Consider a purpose that we have not yet attempted to undertake. At that point the question concerns institutional design: given our purpose, what other features must the institution have or lack in order to be legitimate? The above strategy also presumes that the other features will importantly limit the purposes under question because otherwise the theorizing won't make any headway. For an institution with state-like features, the prima facie case is heavily against its legitimacy and so theorizing legitimacy involves trying to find a potentially legitimating purpose. For more common, benign institutions, the prima face case supports legitimacy, so theorizing is more focused on what purposes (and other features) are delegitimating.

Further, often we do not want to disaggregate institutional purpose from other features as I have so far been doing. For often we are not concerned with institutions defined by their features independent of purpose but with institutional wholes that include purposes. Here institutional purpose is not a hypothetical posit of the theorist but is part and parcel with the sociological description. For example, it makes sense to ask: is the United Nations, given these features including this stated purpose, legitimate here and now? To answer this question, we do need some idea of whether the purpose in question is justifying but we identify the purpose by the fact that it actually is the purpose of an extant institution rather than by its justificatory role. We may not need to identify a hypothetical justifying purpose at all to say that this extant purpose cannot justify the institution as it exists.

Identifying an institutional purpose could be the starting point of our theorizing, the goal, or something in between. How purpose matters for legitimacy depends in part on the variety of ways that judgments of legitimacy are deployed.

Extant purpose

Often we want to work with extant purpose, i.e. what purpose a particular institution undertakes as a descriptive, not prescriptive, matter. This matters most clearly when we ask whether an institution's extant purpose matches a previously identified justifying purpose or when we ask whether a particular institution with this specific extant purpose is legitimate without a fully developed theory of legitimacy for that institution in hand. There are at least four problems when considering extant purpose: the identification, multiple purposes, contestation, and diachronicity problems. They are more pressing in cases beyond the state but arise for theorizing state legitimacy as well.

The first question is how we identify the extant purpose in order to compare it to the justifying purpose. This may not seem like much of a problem: many institutions profess to undertake a specific purpose, for example as articulated in mission statements. The United Nations provides a good example. Article 1 of its charter explicitly lays out four purposes: (1) to maintain international peace and security, (2) to develop friendly relations among nations, (3) to achieve international cooperation in solving international problems and in promoting respect for human rights, and (4) to be a center for harmonizing the actions of nations for these common ends (*Charter* 1945). When looking at the activities of the UN, we can see how many of its actions align with these purposes and how its many subagencies often take pains to explain how their activities forward these aims. It is plausible to accept that these are actually the UN's purposes. Yet it would be exceptionally naïve to simply accept the professed purpose of any given institution.

The Constitution of the Ku Klux Klan declares that the organization desires "to promote patriotism toward our Civil Government; honorable peace among men and nations; protection for and happiness in the homes of our people; manhood, brotherhood, and love among ourselves, and liberty, justice and fraternity among all mankind' (*Constitution* 1921). Yet it is clear that this is not the extant purpose of the KKK. What it declares and what it does are two different things. (This makes sense for institutions with unpopular and impermissible extant purposes, for they will want to hide behind claims to permissible purposes to bolster their claims to legitimacy and to the protections legitimacy provides.) We need a way of identifying extant purpose beyond taking institutions at their word because some institutions do not explicitly profess any purpose and because sometimes there is a mismatch between professed purpose and extant purpose.[15] Call this *the identification problem*.

Second, institutions often have multiple extant purposes. This makes the relationship between the features of the institution and its legitimacy considerably more complicated on its own. But it also raises the possibility that multiple purposes may conflict.[16] The UN, for example, is committed to both the promotion of peace and securing human rights. It structures its institutional norms, roles, and relations between them in order to better achieve its purposes. Yet some features that advance the prospects of peace undercut its ability to secure human rights. The fact that the United States and the Russian Federation each have a veto on the Security Council is important for ensuring their continued participation and so securing peace, but the veto allows each to protect themselves and their allies against UN action addressing human rights violations. Actual institutions often undertake a variety of tasks as a result of a variegated and complicated history and cannot be easily categorized in ways that lend themselves to straightforward evaluations of legitimacy. Call this *the multiple purposes problem*.

The multiple purposes problem and the identification problem interact. What we are mostly concerned with in the identification problem is identifying the constitutive purpose of the institution, the organizing principle that gives it shape. Part of the multiple purposes problem is that institutions might have multiple constitutive purposes. But many institutions also undertake purposes that are not constitutive of the institution. Here further complexities arise. Among the many extant purposes any institution might have, how do we distinguish constitutive from non-constitutive purposes? Under what circumstances does undertaking non-constitutive purposes matter for the legitimacy of an institution, which is mainly a matter of its constitutive purpose? A state may be made illegitimate if it undertakes any non-constitutive purposes, but other kinds of institutions may not, with respect to some non-constitutive purposes but not others.

Third is *the contestation problem*. Institutional purpose, and the degree to which an institution is achieving its purpose, is often contested. Under some circumstances, particularly in the case of political institutions that have as their purpose the representation of all their subjects' interests, contestation is not only a descriptive feature of the institution but is also both ineliminable and desirable. One of the justifying purposes of such institutions is accounting for, and indeed enabling, disagreement and contestation over the shape and structure of the institution itself. But if purposes and their achievement are contested, it is unclear how legitimacy judgments can coordinate practical stances towards institutions in the way required for such judgments to play their distinctive practical role.

Finally, consider *the diachronicity problem*. Actual institutions change over time and their purposes can change as well. How do we identify the extant purpose of an institution when that very thing may be changing over time? Does the fact that an institution had some purpose in the past, and so was shaped by that purpose, matter for its legitimacy now, even if it has changed (e.g. the United States government and white supremacy)? Do we take into account the improvement of extant purpose over time? Do we take into account the possibility of reform in the future? These issues are especially important in light of the practical purpose of legitimacy judgments, which are supposed to coordinate our practical stance with respect to institutions. Our practical stance over time is made more complicated by changing institutional purpose.

One way to address these problems would be to articulate some sort of process by which we could, for example, force institutional participants to commit themselves to a particular purpose. Ultimately, however, while these problems complicate our judgments of legitimacy, I do not think they are problems that can be *solved*. The features of institutions that give rise to these problems are ineliminable: their historical nature, their persistence across time and responsiveness to changing contexts, their inclusion of a wide range of individuals under conditions of reasonable disagreement, and so on.

These problems also arise out of the tensions between various normative and evaluative standards that we need to use to analyze institutions and our relationships to them. Sometimes we are concerned with making new institutions, sometimes our relations to extant institutions, sometimes reforming institutions from the outside, sometimes from the inside. These concerns will weight various features of institutions differently as they consider the various goods and rights of institutions under various presentations. Legitimacy is relevant to all these questions in different ways, as are other modes of evaluation. Any 'solution' to these problems will not be a matter of constructing an institution that avoids them but of applying a more capacious and suitable theory of legitimacy to institutions as we find them.

Conclusion: a way forward?

Traditionally understood, legitimacy requires you to *actively contribute* towards the institution's purpose because obedience (and other weaker forms of support) makes you a part of the coordinated action that constitutes pursuit of the purpose. When that purpose becomes unclear for any of a variety of reasons, the idea that you have an obligation to contribute towards that purpose is called into question. A right to the obedience and support of others is rightfully viewed as very demanding, impinging on self-determination and individual autonomy as obedience and support do, so the purpose at which obedience and support are directed needs to be clear and weighty. On my more minimalist approach, according to which legitimacy just is the right to function and nothing more, the correlated uptake of legitimacy is non-interference rather than contribution. A claim against interference even when it is unclear what purpose one is undertaking is much more palatable than a claim to active contribution and support when the purpose is unclear.

Legitimacy, on my view, creates the space in our social practices for people to come together in organized groups and attempt to achieve certain goals and generate certain goods. We need such a space because the goals and goods of institutions are important and cannot be achieved otherwise; we need legitimacy to coordinate the normative boundaries of such a space because we disagree about what goods matter, to what degree they matter, and what (institutional) means are appropriate for pursuing them. This space is defined not by which institutions we should actively support but which we should not interfere with.

Creating a space in this way is not only amenable to conflicts and questions about institutional purpose; part of the point of such a space is precisely to enable experimenting that is necessarily tentative and unsure. Thus the facts that an institution might not have a clear purpose, might undertake a variety of purposes with conflicting dictums, or might change its purpose over time, are not intrinsically problematic. It is understood to be part of why we need and employ legitimacy discourse as a distinct sort of normative evaluation.

On my view, legitimacy judgments answer a very specific and very fundamental question: do we have to allow this institution to continue? We can coherently answer in the positive even when the problems of institutional purpose arise. Consider the identification problem. If we look at an institution, how it functions, the effects it has, and so on, we may not be able to glean its extant purpose. But this is not a fatal blow for its legitimacy on my view because it may be entitled to non-interference. If the means it uses are not objectionable and if it has few (or no) negative effects, then the fact that we don't know what it's for is not necessarily problematic. But it is hard to see how this could be true when we understand legitimacy to correlate to duties of obedience and support. Parallel points can be made of the other problems: a more minimalist theory of legitimacy of the sort I prefer makes space for accounting for – and even encouraging – complications of institutional purpose, while theories that require active support encounter problems. All I can do here is gesture towards these arguments.

To conclude: institutional purpose matters for legitimacy in a variety of ways. Whether an institution undertakes a morally impermissible, merely permissible, or mandatory purpose matters because it changes the justificatory bar for the institution's right to function in complex ways. Generally speaking, institutions with impermissible purposes have the least normative leeway while institutions with a mandatory purpose have the most. This leeway sets the bar for how other features of the institution matter for its legitimacy: an institution with a mandatory purpose may be able to use harmful or otherwise impermissible means to achieve its purpose, for example.

Institutional purpose is also more complicated once we move beyond the state. For institutional types that are less well-defined and less entrenched in our actual world, we have more questions about purpose. An institution's purpose may change over time, it may be difficult to identify the actual purpose(s) of an institution, these purposes may be contested, and may even conflict. We are concerned with the legitimacy of actual institutional tokens because we want to know how we relate to the institutions that shape our lives. As such, institutional purpose has a variety of roles to play other than as a hypothetical justificatory purpose for an institutional type, the role it plays most prominently in theorizing the state. Due to this, it pays to directly theorize institutional purpose and how it matters for legitimacy as I have here. These considerations can then be combined with our theorizing of other institutional features and how they matter for legitimacy to come to a more plausible and general theory of legitimacy for institutions of all kinds, in every circumstance we encounter them.

Notes

1. See Erman (in press) for a recent attempt to work some similar issues out in the context of particular political purposes.
2. Many institutions also address rules to 'outsiders' or non-members; political institutions are a prime example of this. However, my point here is to define the core of what it means to be an institution and institutions are defined by the rules that define institutional roles and regulate the activities of members. The next step is important for the subclass of institutions that claim to bind outsiders in a particular way, but not for institutions in general.
3. Normative standing is a set of Hohfeldian advantages and disadvantages (Hohfeld, 1919).

4. Thus it will not do to reduce an institution's purpose to a description of its actual functions. We need the purpose to describe the institution itself, but also to identify a mismatch between purpose and how it functions in practice, which may itself matter for legitimacy. Compare Buchanan and Keohane (2006, p. 422) on institutional integrity. Even further, we are often concerned with the prospects for reform when we consider an institution's legitimacy and having a purpose that may not be met but can be a guide for effective reform will matter as well. Thanks to an anonymous reviewer for pushing me to clarify this.
5. This can apply to sub-units; for example, on legislatures, see Waldron (2016, p. 154).
6. This example shows the contrast with the historical approach to individuating institutions. To my mind these distinct individuation criteria are simply useful in different contexts; neither captures the 'real' institution.
7. The right to non-interference is the core of the right to function but depending on the nature of the institutions' functioning, this may well entail further normative advantages, as mentioned in Adams (2018). Thanks to an anonymous reviewer for pressing me to clarify this issue. The important point here is that legitimacy necessarily and minimally includes this element, and that is enough to consider how purpose matters for the stringency of the requirements we would put on an institution achieving this status. Note also that the correlative duty not to interfere is only the duty that correlates to legitimacy; members, outsiders, and others may all well be under a variety of other duties and in general relate to the institution in a variety of ways due to other factors.
8. All institutions depend on free acceptance by some core group of participants. Some institutions, most notably states, also coercively impose roles on people. This is a hugely complicating matter for the legitimacy of such institutions that prima facie defeats the positive case I just outlined.
9. Thanks to an anonymous reviewer for pressing me on this question.
10. This is (at least implicitly) considered throughout this special issue, including by Scherz and Zysset, Christiano, and especially Schmelzle.
11. This is not to endorse a pure libertarian baseline for evaluating institutional legitimacy. For example, we may have good reasons for forbidding certain types of economic institutions because of the effects of allowing the type, despite the fact that any given token might be unobjectionable on its own.
12. For example, in January of 2017 the German Constitutional Court decided not to ban the neo-Nazi NPD party on the grounds that it was ineffective. Thanks to a reviewer for bringing this example to my attention.
13. This strategy is employed whether one thinks that ultimately the outcomes of the state matter most for its legitimacy or the process by which the state comes about (for example by consent) matters most. For even in the latter case, the question is why people would consent to the state *given* some understanding of what the state is for, especially because no plausible account relies on actual extant consent; theories of tacit and hypothetical consent need to reconstruct what counts as consent and what is being consented to. Thanks to an anonymous reviewer for pushing me to clarify this.
14. It may not even work in those cases (Sangiovanni, 2013, p. 221).
15. Furthermore, even sincere statements of institutional purpose can have a variety of aims (Lang & Lopers-Sweetman, 1991).
16. See Pavel, this issue, for consideration of the trade-offs between pursuing different goals in international law.

Disclosure statement

No potential conflict of interest was reported by the author.

ORCID

N. P. Adams http://orcid.org/0000-0001-8580-0872

References

Adams, N. P. (2018). Institutional legitimacy. *The Journal of Political Philosophy*, *26*(1), 84–102.
Buchanan, A. (2013). *The heart of human rights*. Oxford: Oxford University Press.
Buchanan, A., & Keohane, R. O. (2006). The legitimacy of global governance institutions. *Ethics and International Affairs*, *20*(4), 405–437.
Charter of the United Nations, 1945. Retrieved May 20, 2018, from http://www.un.org/en/charter-united-nations/
Collingwood, V., & Logister, L. (2005). State of the art: Addressing the INGO 'Legitimacy Deficit'. *Political Studies Review*, *3*(2), 175–192.
Constitution and Laws of the Knights of the Ku Klux Klan, 1921. Retrieved May 20, 2018, from https://archive.lib.msu.edu/DMC/AmRad/constitutionlawsknights.pdf
Erman, E. (in press). A function-sensitive approach to the political legitimacy of global governance. *British Journal of Political Science*.
Hohfeld, W. N. (1919). *Fundamental legal conceptions as applied to judicial reasoning*. New Haven, CT: Yale University Press.
Lang, D. W., & Lopers-Sweetman, R. (1991). The role of statements of institutional purpose. *Research in Higher Education*, *32*(6), 599–624.
Levy, J. T. (2015). *Rationalism, pluralism, & freedom*. Oxford: Oxford University Press.
Miller, S. (2009). *The moral foundations of social institutions*. Cambridge: Cambridge University Press.
Pettit, P. (1997). *Republicanism*. Oxford: Oxford University Press.
Pogge, T. (2008). *World poverty and human rights* (2nd ed.). Cambridge, MA: Polity Press.
Sangiovanni, A. (2013). Solidarity in the European union. *Oxford Journal of Legal Studies*, *33*(2), 213–241.
Waldron, J. (1981). A right to do wrong. *Ethics*, *92*(1), 21–39.
Waldron, J. (2016). *Political political theory*. Cambridge, MA: Harvard University Press.

ⓐ OPEN ACCESS

Global democracy and feasibility

Eva Erman and Jonathan W. Kuyper

ABSTRACT
While methodological and metatheoretical questions pertaining to feasibility have been intensively discussed in the philosophical literature on justice in recent years, these discussions have not permeated the debate on global democracy. The overall aim of this article is to demonstrate the fruitfulness of importing some of the advancements made in this literature into the debate on global democracy, as well as to develop aspects that are relevant for explaining the role of feasibility in normative political theory. This is done by pursuing two arguments. First, to advance the work on the role of feasibility, we suggest as intuitively plausible two metatheoretical constraints on normative political theorizing – the 'fitness constraint' and the 'functional constraint' – which elucidate a number of aspects relevant in determining proper feasibility constraints for an account in political theory. Secondly, to illustrate the usefulness of this feasibility framework, we sketch an account of global democracy consisting of normative principles which respond differently to these aspects and thus are tied to different feasibility constraints as well as exemplify how it may be applied in practice.

In responding to the challenge of finding solutions to shared political problems that cross nation-state borders, we are witnessing a growing literature on global political legitimacy in international political theory. This has led to numerous attempts to understand what political legitimacy might mean in a global context and what it might require in terms of normative principles or standards. Alongside consent and beneficial consequences, democracy is one of the main normative sources used to theorize political legitimacy. In the debate on global democracy, there has been a tendency to dismiss at the outset more ideal accounts as being too unrealistic to be of interest or of any use at all. Despite this criticism of ideal proposals, critics have themselves been rather silent about which feasibility constraints are tied to their own supposedly more realistic proposals of global democracy. Instead, some underspecified notion of feasibility is either implicitly presumed or articulated but not motivated. This has led to a general confusion with regard to feasibility and the role it plays in theorizing global democracy.[1] Such confusion is unfortunate, given that we can only assess the correctness of an account if we know what it aims to achieve, such as what the proposed normative political principles are supposed to regulate. By contrast, methodological and metatheoretical questions pertaining to feasibility have been intensively discussed in the philosophical literature on feasibility and global justice in recent years. The progress in that field, however, has not made its way into the debate on global democracy in political theory.

To remedy this deficiency and kick-start the debate on the role of feasibility in global democracy, we aim to demonstrate the fruitfulness of importing some of the advancements made in this philosophical literature into the debate on global democracy, as well as to develop aspects that are relevant in explaining the role of feasibility in normative political theory. This is done by pursuing two arguments. First, to respond to the vagueness with regard to feasibility, we suggest as plausible two metatheoretical constraints on normative political theorizing, the 'fitness constraint' and the 'functional constraint', which elucidate a number of aspects relevant in determining proper feasibility constraints of an account in political theory. Secondly, to illustrate the usefulness of this 'feasibility framework', we sketch an account of global democracy consisting of normative principles which respond differently to these aspects and thus are tied to different feasibility constraints as well as exemplify how this framework may be applied in practice.

In developing these arguments, the article unfolds in three sections. First, we briefly present the main conceptual and normative concerns addressed in the philosophical literature on feasibility. Secondly, we undertake a metatheoretical analysis of the two constraints and discuss the aspects they bring forward of relevance when thinking about feasibility. Thirdly, we adopt these constraints and develop an account of global democracy to illustrate the usefulness of this feasibility framework.

Feasibility: some conceptual remarks

There is no consensus in the debate as to how the very concept of 'feasibility' should be used.[2] Indeed, it is doubtful whether we can offer a meaningful answer without a clear sense of what the consequences of feasibility (or lack thereof) are supposed to entail. Thus, how feasibility is understood depends on the different roles that feasibility claims play in political theory. As we understand it, the basic idea is a more demanding constraint on normative theory than the classical 'ought implies can' proviso. Whereas the 'ought implies can' proviso filters out those normative accounts that for some reason or other cannot be realized, the role of (in)feasibility considerations is an additional requirement. In general terms, this requirement is captured by Nicholas Southwood's 'ought-implies-feasible' proviso:

> (OF) An agent X ought to realize a state of affairs O only if it is feasible for X to realize O (Southwood, 2016, p. 9; see also Southwood & Wiens, 2016, p. 3043).[3]

This proviso captures two important aspects of feasibility claims in normative theory: they are agent-relative and an obligation is conditioned on feasibility, i.e. it is necessary, but not sufficient, that it is feasible to realize a state of affairs. But additional aspects are important in understanding feasibility claims, helpfully explicated by Pablo Gilabert and Holly Lawford-Smith's schema:

> (F) It is feasible for X to φ to bring about O in Z

On this analysis, claims about feasibility involve a four-place predicate as to what a given agent X can do (a set of actions φ) to achieve a state of affairs O in a given context Z, where the context itself also includes feasibility-affecting considerations (Gilabert & Lawford-Smith, 2012, p. 812).[4] An important aspect of the notion of feasibility in this schema is the set of actions sought to bring about an outcome, which suggests an *intentional* component. In line with other theorists, we find it plausible to assume that the concept of feasibility applies only to the (possible) realization of a state of affairs through intentional actions by agents (Southwood & Wiens, 2016, p. 3041, n. 6). Natural events giving rise to certain states of affairs thus fall outside its domain of application and so it would not be meaningful to ask whether heavy rainfall today is feasible or infeasible (Erman & Möller, 2019).

A virtue of the 'ought-implies-feasible' proviso, together with this schema, is that they make explicit the basic components of feasibility and thus render immediately problematic the oversimplification and lack of clarity too often present in the literature on global democracy, where most of the four components of the predicate are left unspecified. In this literature, critics of ambitious accounts of global democracy, such as cosmopolitan democracy, routinely deride these proposals as being unfeasible, lauding their own as being feasible. For example, Robert Dahl insisted that international organizations (IOs) could not live up to standards of democracy because the global system lacks the kinds of shared collective identity and common political culture necessary for domestic democracy (Dahl, 1999). Ruth Grant and Robert Keohane argue that IOs specifically – and world politics more generally – cannot be democratic. In their view, 'the fact that global democracy is infeasible' means that domestic democracy remains important (Grant & Keohane, 2005, p. 40). In these instances, the agents, actions, states of affairs, and contexts underpinning proposals are rarely specified and never contrasted against (supposedly) less feasible alternatives.

With regard to the content of feasibility, philosophers agree that the feasibility of – for example – an ideal state of affairs depends on whether or not there is a *trajectory* leading to it from the present state of affairs, i.e. whether or not there is an accessible path of actions that we can take from our starting-point to arrive at the sought after state of affairs (Gilabert & Lawford-Smith, 2012, p. 813). The disagreement begins when we consider what should count as 'accessible', which has to do with how we interpret 'feasible' in the proviso (OF) above. For example, theorists have argued that feasibility should be understood in terms of probability (Lawford-Smith 2013), conditional ability (Estlund, 2011, 2014), possibility (Gheaus, 2013), restricted possibility (Wiens, 2015), rational-volitional capacity (Southwood, 2016), or costliness (Räikkä, 1998).

In our view, these disagreements about how best to understand feasibility directly reflects the heterogeneity of normative political theory. Political theories have myriad aims and goals, contexts and delimitations, and we think that there are no general answers to best understand feasibility (Erman & Möller, 2018). As we will argue below, whether feasibility is best understood in terms of, say, conditional ability or costliness depends on what an intended normative political principle aims to regulate (functional constraint) and how it fits together with the other principles, values and states of affairs which are endorsed in the account (fitness constraint) (Erman & Möller, 2019).

Two constraints and aspects of relevance for feasibility

The role of feasibility in the literature on global democracy is undertheorized. It is evident that, in recent years, philosophical discussions about feasibility and methodological discussions in the debate on ideal and non-ideal theory have not made an imprint on this literature.[5] This is unfortunate, given the progress that has been made in the field. As mentioned in the introduction, the overall aim of this article is to demonstrate the profitability of importing some of these discussions into the debate on global democracy and more importantly, to refine aspects that are relevant for understanding the role of feasibility in normative political theory. In this section, we do the latter by suggesting two metatheoretical constraints on normative theorizing – the fitness constraint and the functional constraint – through which we propose four relevant aspects for determining proper feasibility constraints of an account in political theory, together constituting a 'feasibility framework'. According to this framework, there is no general, pre-theoretical answer as to which feasibility constraints are most appropriately tied to a normative political principle or account; rather, this depends on the context of the particular theory in question (its aim, and so on).

The functional constraint

In its most abstract form, the functional constraint is the requirement that the guiding principles of a normative account must be appropriate for the aims of the account – that is, what the suggested principles are supposed to regulate, and the limits within which they are supposed to function. The constraint involves three aspects of importance in determining appropriate feasibility constraints of an account: the principle-kind aspect; the practice-kind aspect; and the temporal aspect.

The *principle-kind aspect* concerns what sort of principle it is. Political theorists commonly argue for a principle of justice, a principle of fairness, a principle of democracy, a principle of legitimacy, or the like. The principle-kind aspect has consequences for the kind of feasibility considerations, and how they become appropriate, in at least two ways. First, for a principle to be feasible, it must be able to be interpreted as a principle of the intended kind. If the sought principle is a principle of justice, it arguably cannot be a principle which suggests that all goods should be distributed to, say, persons with large hands, or something similarly arbitrary. Second, when specifying what kind of principle is intended, it is important to determine whether it is supposed to have direct or indirect application – that is, whether or not its function is directly action-guiding or 'merely' indirectly so. Many critics of ideal accounts of global democracy take feasibility to entail direct action-guidance in the sense that it should be immediately possible to act in accordance with the principle. However, this demand neglects several indirect ways of guiding action.

A model, for example, is by definition similar in important respects to the phenomenon of interest and includes some counterfactual assumptions and simplifications which set it apart from the real phenomenon. But a model of, say, a power plant may still be helpful for the design of a control system for the power plant. Similarly, the aim of more or less ideal theories of global democracy is to supply a model case for our actual society. Assuming features that no actual society may ever exemplify might be seen exactly as a model of an actual society.

The *practice-kind aspect* of the functional constraint concerns the target of the principle, i.e. to what practice the principle is supposed to be applied (c.f. Adams this issue). As worded by Charles Beitz, since normative political principles are supposed to regulate the conduct and structure of a practice, any candidate principle for this practice must be 'formulated in such a way that it satisfies a condition of applicability' (Beitz, 2014, p. 227). Consider, for example, the potential difference between a principle of democracy for regulating some decisions at the university and a principle of democracy for society at large. Importantly, the practice-kind aspect involves a 'target flexibility' that is often neglected in the literature on global democracy. One dimension of this flexibility concerns criteria for a practice-kind, that is, what counts as belonging to the practice. Typically, the practice that an intended principle is supposed to regulate allows for a certain amount of flexibility, both with regard to what qualifies as the practice in question as well as the 'borders' of this practice, which is usually negotiable.

Critics of ambitious theories of global democracy often reject them on the grounds that they cannot regulate the kind of practice intended. Instead, it is assumed that existing practices set the limits as to what is required for democracy. As argued by John Dryzek and Simon Niemeyer, for example, discursive forms of democratic representation are preferable to electoral representation on the grounds that it is 'sometimes feasible when the representation of persons is not so feasible (especially in transnational settings lacking a well-defined demos)' (Dryzek & Niemeyer, 2008, p. 481).

But such proposals neglect another dimension of target flexibility, and that is the issue of how potential deviations from the sought target practice should be handled. Let us assume, for example, that the aim of the theorist is to develop a democratic theory for the European Union (EU). Suppose that the theorist finds that true democracy would demand that the EU was a fiscal union. But the EU is *not* a fiscal union, and a critic could therefore argue that the theorist's principle, however justified for a fiscal union, cannot be a principle for the EU.[6] The theorist has two basic ways of responding to this concern. First, she may contest the conceptual claim, arguing that even if changed to a fiscal union, it would still be the European Union. This option utilizes an aspect of the target flexibility mentioned above, according to which the borders of the target practice are negotiable. Secondly, she may accept the current constitution of the EU as a necessary constraint on her theory, acknowledging that her account cannot be an account for the EU. Importantly, though, and neglected in the debate on global democracy, the latter option entails an open question that depends specifically on what *function* the account aims to fulfil (see also Adams this issue). The theorist may conclude that if her account of democracy is not compatible with the target practice, *so much the worse for the target practice*. In other words, given her aim with the account, what matters might be that there is a *possible* arrangement playing the (approximate) *role* of the EU in which democracy may be upheld, not that the institution is constituted in the same way as the current EU (Erman & Möller, 2018, 2019).

The *temporal aspect* of the functional constraint concerns the extent to which a normative principle or account is primarily present-directed or future-directed. In other words, whether or not a principle is feasible strongly depends on *when* the principle is supposed to come into effect. If the function of the principle is to regulate current state of affairs, the feasibility constraints are typically set by the present empirical context of the target practice. For example, the present set of resources we have at our disposal – our present aims, desires and skillsets – will set limits as to what is possible to achieve at present, and the principles for today need to accommodate (some of) these facts. If the function of the principle is to regulate an end-state or ideal practice, however, the feasibility constraints could be much more open-ended. The upper limits for feasibility are then given not by our presently available goods and resources, and people's present aims, desires and skillsets, but by what is possible to reach, given the present *starting-point*.

Indeed, between these two extremes there is an endless number of possible time-frames which delimit the feasibility space for a guiding principle. However, recall that feasibility considerations are considerations about *trajectory* in all of these cases, pointing to an accessible path of actions that can be taken to arrive at the desired state of affairs. It must thus be possible to move in incremental steps from the (typically less ideal) present state of affairs to the (more ideal) states that the principles directly regulate. This is not to say that the theorist, in order to justify her account, must *demonstrate* that the future world is reachable. Of course, if it can be demonstrated that the world is *not* reachable from the present world, then an account aiming to be directly applicable has problems. But as long as the case is *inconclusive*, which it often is when it comes to human nature and empirical circumstances in the future, uncertainty about whether or not circumstances – in which suggested principles are both applicable and justifiable – are possible to reach within the constraints set by the temporal aspect is *not* sufficient to reject the account.[7]

The fitness constraint

Whilst the functional constraint is context-dependent, the fitness constraint is a requirement of the relation between the commitments made in an account. Being essentially a coherence condition, the fitness constraint may seem 'trivial' or 'self-evident', with little practical import for political theorizing. However, we believe that it has implications for feasibility that are often ignored and therefore deserve more attention than many theorists acknowledge. The fitness constraint involves one aspect of particular importance in determining what kind of feasibility considerations become appropriate: the dynamic aspect.

The fitness constraint puts a *dynamic* condition on the principle that the account sets out to justify. Any direction of justification is allowed, whether bottom up or top down, or a set of commitments on an equal level of prior justificatory force. This is the case because the fitness constraint concerns the ways in which *all* relevant claims fit together in the account. Simply put, in order for the account to be justified, it must fit with the other claims on which the account is premised. If there appears to be tensions between different commitments of the account, regardless of other virtues, they must be resolved before the account may be considered justified. And the resolution may only be made in either one, or a combination of two, fundamental ways: by abandoning at least one of the commitments in the account, or by showing that there actually is no tension after all (Erman & Möller, 2018).

Given its formal character, we believe that few theorists would reject the fitness constraint. Yet, its dynamic aspect is surprisingly underappreciated. In several current debates, arguments are often worked out as if justifications have a set direction, not only in the literature on global democracy but also in the justice literature. Consider, for example, the debate on ideal and non-ideal theory, in which non-ideal theorists insist that we defy the 'top down' strategy utilized by ideal theorists – starting with general higher-level principles – and instead work in a context-sensitive 'bottom up' manner when we theorize appropriate principles of justice (Farrelly, 2007; Mills, 2005). Likewise, in the debate on practice-independence and practice-dependence, practice-dependent theorists insist that the justification of a principle of justice is dependent on the nature of the practice it is intended to govern and that we may only get a proper understanding of this nature through a robust interpretive methodology (Ronzoni, 2009; Sangiovanni, 2008). There is thus a tendency to assume that the endorsement of the proposition 'q justifies p' would also imply the denial of its converse, i.e. that 'p justifies q'.

Importantly, though, the dynamic aspect suggests that different feasibility considerations may be appropriate for different principles *within* an account, depending on how the principles harmonize. Even a typical ideal account could comprise more or less ideal principles. For example, a democratic theory may consist of a principle of democracy which is construed under the constraint that it must be realizable within the long-term future and a higher-level moral principle that does not set out such feasibility demands. Similarly, a non-ideal account may consist of more or less realizable principles, for example, one regulating what democracy requires under current socio-political conditions and given available resources, another aimed at reducing severely undemocratic practices. Recalling what the functional constraint requires, the appropriate feasibility considerations for each principle is dependent on what the principle is aimed to achieve (see also Adams this issue; Scherz and Zysset this issue). And there are no predetermined limits to functional variety within an account nor to the number of principles it may incorporate, as long as the principles harmonize so that the fitness constraint is fulfilled. In a nutshell, this means that if an account includes an applied principle construed under demanding feasibility constraints, and a more general higher-level principle construed under weaker or no feasibility constraints, the applied principle must be reasonable from the standpoint of the higher-level principle *given* the feasibility constraints assumed by the applied principle (and vice versa) (Erman & Möller, 2019).

Global democracy and feasibility considerations

So far we have focused on our first argument, responding to the vagueness with regard to the role of feasibility in normative theorizing, by suggesting two metatheoretical constraints, which together involve four aspects that are important in determining appropriate feasibility constraints of an account. In this final section, we will pursue our second argument by illustrating how this feasibility framework might be used in theorizing the contours of an account of global democracy. By 'contours' we mean an account consisting of principles we see as central for global democracy, but where no claims are made about them being necessary or jointly sufficient. As will become evident below, we focus on one indispensable aspect of democracy, namely, political decision-making. Without doubt, many other aspects would have to be theorized to develop a fully fledged account of global democracy. However decision-making is often considered the most essential function of democracy since it lies at the heart of what is meant by 'the rule by the people', i.e. the idea that those who are supposed to abide by the rules also should be the authors of them.

Of course, the feasibility framework as such can neither lend any support for our suggested account nor solve any substantive matters with regard to global democracy, since it is constituted by metatheoretical conditions. However, it can be applied to demonstrate the rich array of possibilities available for the theorist with regard to feasibility considerations. Thus, given that the purpose of this section is not to contribute a first-order theory but to illustrate the usefulness of the feasibility framework, we will not spend much time on the kinds of justification needed to defend the suggested principles of the account. Instead, we begin by introducing the three principles (P1-P3), thereafter explicating their feasibility constraints in response to the four aspects, followed by an application of the applied principle (P3) to empirical circumstances.

Three normative political principles

Our skeleton account of global democracy consists of three principles. Let us start by introducing them:

(P1) *The all-affected principle*: All those persons who are significantly affected by a public decision have a moral right to due consideration.[8]

(P2) *The equal say principle*: All and only those agents who are subjected to a system of laws have an equal say in the decision-making about its basic form and the overarching societal goals and aims.

(P3) *The rightful capacity to impact principle*: All agents with the rightful capacity to impact the decision-making process, to level out inequalities, should do so.

Both the all-affected principle (P1) and the equal say principle (P2) are intermediary normative political principles in the proposed scheme, rather than what is sometimes referred to as foundational or higher-level principles.[9] Whilst P1 constitutes a *fairness* principle with the aim of regulating political decision-making in general, P2 is a robust *democratic* principle with the aim of regulating law-making specifically.[10]

Both principles are tied to two weak feasibility conditions, demanding that a principle be compatible with the basic features of human nature as we know it and possible to achieve from the status quo (see Buchanan, 2004). These conditions understand feasibility in terms of conditional ability (Estlund, 2011).

One might ask why P2, given its narrower scope, is conditioned by the same weak feasibility constraints as P1. Importantly, though, a narrower scope does not necessitate more demanding feasibility conditions. Rather, in line with our metatheoretical discussion, it is the function of the principle – what the principle sets out to regulate – which is decisive. Responding to the temporal aspect of the functional constraint by building into a principle regulating law-making the requirement that it must be achievable within the near future, or that it must take into consideration exactly how current laws are made, would just taint it with a status quo bias that is unjustified given its role as an intermediary principle. Why settle for a less democratic cut-off point when we theorize what is required of law-making in order for it to be democratic?

This justification concerns the practice-kind aspect, in particular its target flexibility, which raises questions about the *limits* of feasibility. When feasibility considerations are made in the current literature, it is typically the 'upper limit' that is discussed: if the suggested principles demand too much of people, the account is not feasible. But on our functional constraint, the question of a 'lower limit' is equally important. If an account of democracy demands too little of people, the account is equally infeasible *as an account of democracy*. This would mean that, rather than attempting to find a bar of 'democracy' low enough to be compatible with, say, the practice of slavery, abolishing the practice in its entirety seems to be the better alternative (see Erman & Möller, 2019).

Let us now compare the aim of the intermediary equal say principle (P2) with the aim of the rightful capacity to impact principle (P3), which is the most applied principle in our scheme. The aim of P3 is *distributive* in the sense that it is intended to level out the unequal distribution of decision-making power in the global domain to strengthen the prerequisites for approximating the all-affected principle (P1) and the equal say principle (P2), and thus realizing global democracy. To have 'rightful capacity' requires that three criteria are fulfilled: that an agent (a) has justified aims (i.e. to strengthen the prerequisites for realizing P1 and P2); (b) is sufficiently capable of promoting the inclusion of wrongly excluded individuals and groups in global politics (i.e. those who are not given a right to due consideration even though they are significantly affected and those who do not have a say in the law-making even though they are subjected to the system of laws); and (c) has a capacity with no 'tainted origins', i.e. a capacity built through moral wrongdoings (Buchanan, 2013, pp. 188–89). P3 is theorized under feasibility conditions which require that a principle is applicable to global governance arrangements under current conditions and with current resources, with the likelihood of being at least partially realized within a couple of generations. Feasibility is here understood in terms of psychological and material costliness.

Needless to say, a fully fledged theory of global democracy would have to specify this in more detail as well as accommodate further principles for regulating functions other than decision-making. But this scheme of principles suffices to illustrate the usefulness of the sketched feasibility framework. Consider first the functional constraint. To begin with, the three principles differ with regard to the *principle-kind aspect*. One aims to achieve procedural fairness (P1), a second aims to achieve democratic legitimacy through political equality (P2), and a third is distributive and aims to level out unequal decision-making power (P3). Moreover, concerning the *practice-kind aspect*, one is construed to be applied to political decision-making generally (P1), a second is construed to be applicable to law-making (P2), and a third is construed to be applicable to unequal power relations in the political domain (P3). Finally, with regard to the *temporal aspect*, which is particularly important for elaborating appropriate feasibility constraints, two of the principles are ideal-theoretical in the sense that they set out a (possible but demanding) long-term goal (P1 and P2), allowing us to tie them to weak feasibility constraints. The third principle is non-ideal in the sense that the temporal horizon is much more limited (P3). In sum, they have different aims, different domains of application, different levels of applicability, and vary in content and scope.

Let us move from the functional constraint to the fitness constraint. Concerning the *dynamic aspect*, it is quite easy to see the fitness between the principles in one justificatory direction, at least with regard to how the equal say principle (P2) is an application and specification of the all-affected principle (P1) in contexts of law-making, while the rightful capacity to impact principle (P3) is an application and specification of the equal say principle (P2) under current non-ideal conditions.[11] But the fitness condition concerns the whole 'web of commitments' and it is less straightforward how the rightful capacity to impact principle (P3) is a specification of the all-affected principle (P1), since the latter is quite general. Our argument here is that, whilst there are many ways of giving those significantly affected a moral right to due consideration, one *central* way of doing so that is of particular importance *from the standpoint of democracy* is to give them equalized access to the political decision-making by levelling out the distribution of decision power.

The other justificatory direction comes to the fore once we take into account the three aspects of the functional constraint. The equal say principle (P2) is reasonable from the standpoint of the all-affected principle (P1) *given* that P2 is supposed to regulate a kind of decision-making with specific constitutive features. And the rightful capacity to impact principle (P3) is reasonable from the standpoint of P1 and P2 *given* what P3 is intended to do and that it is supposed to be applied to current global governance arrangements (and be partially achievable within a couple of generations). Hence, the principles give each other support and fit together in a way that the fitness constraint requires:

$$P1 \leftrightarrow P2 \leftrightarrow P3$$

Note from the above analysis that the level of application of a principle, which decides whether it is an intermediary or an applied principle, is not decided by justificatory force but by aim, domain of application, and temporal horizon. Hence, the level of application is a relational matter: an intermediary principle may be an applied principle in another scheme, and so on. Indeed, one may think that the proposed scheme necessarily makes P1 justificatory prior – similar to G. A. Cohen's famous justificatory chain of principles (2003) – and in some contexts this may well be the case. However, the fitness constraint is a formal constraint and as such neutral vis-à-vis coherentist and foundationalist theories in epistemology, so specifying and defending a justificatory priority among principles of an account is not mandatory. The fitness constraint only requires that the principles fit together such that they constitute a coherent whole and thus can be justified from the standpoint of one another *given* the feasibility constraints to which they are tied.

Realizing global democracy

As mentioned in the introduction, to evaluate the correctness of a normative political principle we must know to which feasibility constraints it is tied. Among other eventual factual premises, these feasibility constraints constitute an *empirical premise* of the principle. Hence, if the empirical premise turns out to be false, we have good reasons to reject the principle. While the all-affected principle (P1) and the equal say principle (P2) in our scheme are possible to refute on empirical grounds, this would be a tremendously difficult task, given the weak feasibility constraints that they must be compatible with the basic features of human nature as we know it and possible to achieve from the status quo. Yet, these kinds of principles are often rejected outright in the literature on global democracy, for example, because they presumably require a global demos or fulfil some other empirical premise (Miller, 2010; for a critique, see Valentini, 2014). But such charges do not have a bite on these principles (at least not insofar as the feasibility constraints utilized here are presumed). The rightful capacity to impact principle (P3), however, may be rejected on empirical grounds if it turns out to be unlikely to be partially realized within a couple of generations. To illustrate the kind of considerations one would have to make in testing the correctness of this principle, as well as discuss the different ways it may be realized to verify it, let us focus on two empirical examples.

We first need to specify the types of feasibility constraints that we have in mind and which proposals for realizing P3 could be construed. As we saw above, P3 must be applicable under current conditions and with current resources, where feasibility is understood in terms of psychological and material costliness. Due to space limitations, however, we focus our analysis on the material resources necessary for the instantiation of the said proposals, by which we mean economic properties in the form of labour, capital, and technology.

There are also substantial reasons for focusing on material aspects of feasibility in construing a non-ideal principle rather than the more common focus on psychological aspects such as motivation (e.g. political will). First, the literature on feasibility is unclear about the status of psychological constraints (Gilabert & Lawford-Smith, 2012). On one hand, it seems strange to let agents off the moral hook just because an action might be mentally difficult. On the other, persistent and deep cognitive biases do run through (almost) all agents which condition capacity for action. Given this lack of clarity, we will leave the topic for future research. Second, and relatedly, our focus on material conditions does not undermine the importance of thinking through other feasibility constraints, such as psychological ones. However, as our example is illustrative rather than exhaustive, we take it that showing how the feasibility framework can be applied to debates on global democracy suffices to show its merit.

Though somewhat stylized, recent literature on global democracy circulates around two nodes: a civil society view and a statist view (Besson & Martí, in press; for a similar comparative distinction, see Scherz and Zysset this issue; Buchanan & Keohane, 2006). The former, often inspired by Habermasian accounts, puts democratizing faith in civil society organizations to act as representatives for different peoples.[12] This approach sees civil society as either exercising international decision-making in democratic ways, or fixing the democratic deficits created by states through representation in the policy process of IOs (Bohman, 2007; Dryzek, 2012; Macdonald, 2008). The latter view, operating in a Kantian vein, suggests that a principle of state consent should ground a global democracy in which democratic states – *qua* representatives of their citizens – construct international laws, treaties, and IOs that bind states and their citizenry (Christiano, 2015; Moravcsik, 2004).

The civil society view has been a dominant thread in recent global democratic thought. Unpacked more fully, this view sees civil society actors exercising a 'rightful capacity' to represent excluded groups in global law- and policy-making. This can occur in two distinct ways: by representation of groups in the policy processes of IOs, or by representation in private governance initiatives and transnational networks that have authoritative capacity. Though often left unspoken, the rationale for this model is one of feasibility: we already see the involvement of non-state actors in virtually every international regime (i.e. policy area) and almost all major IOs (Steffek, 2013; Tallberg, Sommerer, Squatrito, & Jönsson, 2013). Moreover, the rise of non-state actors in IO policy processes has been complemented by a growing role of non-state actors as private governors, networked collaborators, watchdogs from outside formal IO structures, and organizers of protests and other civic actions.

These myriad roles go some way toward realizing P3 under fairly demanding feasibility constraints. States are not all democratic, and will not be so in the foreseeable future. Citizens of non-democratic states therefore need a vehicle of representation on the international stage, and, reciprocally, IOs require alternate ways to take consideration of the views of all those subjected to laws and all those who are significantly affected by law and policy. Civil society (acting as representatives of excluded groups) offers a tractable response to this problem, even if non-democratic states are often reticent to allow non-state actor access on the ground in those states. Non-state actors can represent excluded groups in IO agenda setting, research, policy formulation, decision-making, as well as implementation and evaluation of decisions (Steffek, 2013). This is crucial for feasibility reasons: IOs do not have unlimited human, financial, or technological resources to reach out and gather views from excluded groups. Staff numbers are oftentimes short, budgets constrained by national governments, and technology lacking to reach those excluded in developing and authoritarian states. In this sense, non-state actors exercise their rightful capacity to impact the decision-making by helping to include the views of those wrongfully excluded.

In a similar way, the rise of private governance initiatives and transnational networks offer a mode for individuals to be represented in international law-making as these bodies craft rules directly. These bodies often emerge in governance gaps where states fail to enact rules or when states do make rules but exclude groups from the process (Green 2013). Again, precisely because IOs and states often exclude groups of people, this approach offers a feasible way to include those excluded (say, by drafting certification initiatives that consider how vulnerable groups are treated in supply chains). This model also already has empirical bite, though to be sure there are still feasibility concerns in realizing P3. Private actors are typically located in the Global North, and questions are raised over their ability to represent those distantly located (Scholte, 2014). Moreover, private bodies also lack staff, money, and technology to systematically represent all groups significantly affected by their rules.

This civil society view is often contrasted against a statist model (or state consent view). On this score, state governments act as the primary representative of different people (typically, their citizenry) in law-making beyond the state. In some ways, this model is also attractive due to its feasibility. State governments have provided the context and backdrop for international law to develop over the past two centuries. The proliferation of IOs with legal authority has occurred through the delegation and pooling activities of state governments (Hooghe & Marks, 2015). Obligations to follow IO decisions and treaty regimes are therefore not imposed on states, but rather voluntarily accepted (i.e. consented to). By representing citizens in the formation and exercise of international authority, democratic legitimacy is maintained as those citizens – through chains of delegation – empower their government who in turn empower international authority-wielders (which can be revoked later if the *demos* wills it).

Proponents of this model are quick to note that state consent remains the key mechanism for rendering international authority democratic. In Thomas Christiano's words, states remain 'the most important institutional mechanism for making large scale political entities directly accountable to people' (2015, p. 7). Additionally, these advocates often deride the importance of civil society efforts. Much of the work engaged in by civil society, so it is said, is part of soft or administrative law, and therefore not a source of international law *stricto sensu* in the same way as treaty or customary international law (Besson & Martí, in press). Finally, advocates argue that sovereignty combined with consent mean that the citizens of small states are given equal voice in the process of international law-making, helping to overcome inter-state imbalances.

The feasibility of this model in cashing out P3 can be criticized, however. Not all states are democratic, and citizens of those states are not able to sanction their representatives (thus breaking the democratic chains of delegation).[13] Some civil society actors now certainly exercise forms of international legal authority viewed as binding over its addressees, and IO policy processes are sometimes captured by special interest groups (Braithwaite & Drahos, 2000). Lastly, while the practice of inter-state negotiations may be formally equal (a disputable claim), they are certainly rife with informal imbalances in terms of resources. Smaller states have less access to information, an inability to send large delegations to international treaty negotiations, less technological ability to collect their own citizens' views, and so on. Given that many states will remain undemocratic in the foreseeable future, and that weak states do not have the money, time, or technology to compete with stronger states in the formation of international law, the notion that a statist model approximates P3 is dubious.

Yet statist proponents are correct to note that the source of international law is predominantly – and, with some exceptions, will remain for generations to come – state consent. Given this impasse, we suggest that viewing the civil society model and state model together is productive in realizing P3. Few scholars opt for either side of this debate *tout court* (though some do), yet how the positions can be combined in realizing normative principles remains underspecified. Most clearly from our analysis, it is evident that states and state-backed IOs have a crucial role to play in crafting international law in democratic ways as representatives of their citizens. But this cannot occur without civil society actors helping to include the views of under-represented groups in the policy process of negotiations. Similarly, non-state actors can help level out negotiation imbalances by providing weaker states with information, acting as pro bono advisors and negotiators, and helping to reduce compliance costs through monitoring implementation of international laws.

Inversely, IOs and states – much more so than civil society – are in a position to help non-democratic states' transition toward democracy. This is a crucial step in ensuring actors from different states exercise their rightful capacity to represent all those bound by international laws. Keohane, Macedo, and Moravcsik have argued that IOs specifically – and multilateralism in general – have net democratic benefits: while it might mean that IOs gain some authority at the expense of governments, these same IOs promote individual rights, restrict special interests, and improve parliamentary deliberation (Keohane, Macedo, & Moravcsik, 2009). Because not all civil society actors are necessarily 'good' democratic representatives, restricting overly-represented groups that might crowd out more vulnerable ones is a step toward realizing P3. In a complementary way, Tallberg and his colleagues have shown that having a high rate of democratic states in an IO membership-pool greatly enhances its openness to civil society activity in the policy process (Tallberg, Sommerer, & Squatrito, 2016). This highlights the symbiosis between an IO's ability to help democratize states, and civil society's ability to contribute more deeply to IOs' decision-making. Given restrictions in resources, combining the civil society and statist views is therefore more fruitful for the realization of P3 than either view on its own.

This argument can be made precisely because of the methodological commitments allowed by the feasibility framework. Many scholars who advocate global democracy pitch their institutional prescription at a higher level, closer to P2 in which their model immediately seeks to cash out the equal say principle (or some version of it). In this way, advocates tend to err and see the civil society model and the statist model as contending candidates. However, by specifying how these two views can embody P3 and 'fit' with P1 and P2 – as well as outlining some feasibility constraints that determine how the proposals can be made functional –

we open up space to combine the two in useful ways. We are able to see the strengths and weaknesses of both models in enacting P3, and develop prescriptions – under the given feasibility constraints – that allow the strengths of one to compensate for the weaknesses of the other.

Conclusion

In this article, we have drawn upon the philosophical literature on feasibility as well as the methodological debates in the justice literature and suggested two metatheoretical constraints, which bring forward four aspects of importance in determining proper feasibility constraints of an account in political theory. In order to show the promise of this framework, we have outlined how it can be used to identify different principles that an account of global democracy may comprise, different 'levels' at which these principles work, and how they fit together. We have then turned toward analyzing two prominent models of global democracy – a civil society view and a statist view – and shown their limitations in light of certain feasibility considerations accompanying the rightful capacity to impact principle (P3). The feasibility framework here allowed us to make a comparative analysis and highlight how the views might be reconciled in attaining P3 in productive ways.

In sum, the article outlines a feasibility framework for the construction of normative principles and proposals, demonstrates its fruitfulness in evaluating two prescriptions, and brings new considerations of feasibility to global democracy scholarship. Indeed, as mentioned at the outset and demonstrated throughout, democracy is only one normative source that may be utilized when theorizing political legitimacy in the global domain. In line with our suggested feasibility framework, the appropriate principle for regulating a certain practice depends on what the principle is supposed to regulate and to what kind of practice it is meant to be applied (as well as within what time-frame). By showing why democracy is important in some set of cases, and relating it to feasibility, we have advanced the literature on global democracy, taken the wider discussions about political legitimacy in global politics a step forward, and contributed to a broader dialogue about feasibility in normative political theory.

Notes

1. For exceptions with regard to vagueness about feasibility in the global democracy literature, see Ulaş (2016) and Valentini (2014).
2. This section draws heavily on Erman & Möller, 2019, where one finds a more developed analysis of feasibility and the two metatheoretical constraints, albeit not in relation to global democracy (see also Erman & Möller, 2018, Ch. 7).
3. 'Agent' does not necessarily (and in political theory not even typically) entail a single person, but can be a group of persons, an institution and the like.

4. Furthermore, it has also been argued that a sought state of affairs must be relatively stable to be feasible (Cohen, 2009, pp. 56–57; Rawls, 1999, pp. 440–41).
5. For literature on ideal and non-ideal theory, (see for example Simmons, 2010; Mills, 2005; Farrelly 2007; Valentini, 2012; Sen, 2009; Schmidtz, 2011; Erman & Möller, 2013).
6. This line of argument – to let the nature of the target practice play an essential role for normative political principles – is common among proponents of practice-dependence in the justice literature (Ronzoni, 2009; Sangiovanni, 2008).
7. This point is similar to Christian Barry and Laura Valentini's note that reasonable disagreement about the feasibility of principles is not sufficient to reject a principle (Barry & Valentini, 2009: 510–11).
8. Note that P1 does not say that *only* those who are significantly affected have a moral right to due consideration. It thus leaves open the case for including others on other grounds (e.g. children who are not significantly affected but for other reasons should have this moral right).
9. However, if one wished to give further justificatory support for the account as a whole, one could well include such a principle, say, a principle of equal respect for persons (e.g. labelled P0 in the scheme), aiming at regulating individual conduct between persons (practice-kind aspect) and perhaps construed under no feasibility constraints and thus, similar to fundamental principles in general, constituting what is sometimes called a 'fact-insensitive' principle (Cohen, 2003).
10. It is worth noting that the suggested feasibility framework allows us to see two allegedly competing criteria of inclusion – the so-called 'all affected principle' and the 'all subjected' principle – as compatible and as giving each other support. On our construal, being significantly affected by a decision does not ground a democratic say because there is no intrinsic connection between being affected in general and having a democratic say (Abizadeh, 2012; Owen, 2012). However, it grounds a moral right to due consideration. By contrast, being subjected to a system of laws does ground a democratic say (here in the form of P2). In our view, the 'all subjected' form of P2 is fitting for regulating law-making because it is able to capture the idea of autonomy as self-rule underpinning democracy, which says that we should only comply with the system of laws that we ourselves have authored. While being affected need not undermine autonomy as self-rule, being coercively and/or legally subjected does. Of course, the feasibility framework as such does not give support these arguments, as they must be settled on *substantive* rather than metatheoretical grounds. However, we illustrate how the framework opens up the possibility space for such arguments.
11. As noted in footnote 9 we might give the all-affected principle (P1) further justificatory support by demonstrating how it is an application and specification of a higher-level moral principle of some kind, such as the equal respect principle (P0) in contexts of decision-making.
12. This view is also congruent with the notion of 'constituent power' that has become more important in debates over democratic deficits at the EU and global level.
13. Of course, even well-developed democratic states have representational deficits due to how political systems weight votes.

Acknowledgments

The authors owe special thanks to the participants of the conference "Legitimacy Beyond the State: Normative and Conceptual Questions" in Bad Homburg (January 2017), in particular Nate Adams, Antoinette Scherz and Cord Schmelzle. In addition, Eva Erman thanks the Swedish Research Council as well as the Marianne and Marcus Wallenberg Foundation for the generous funding of her research, and Jonathan Kuyper thanks Riksbankens Jubileumsfond for the same generosity.

Disclosure statement

No potential conflict of interest was reported by the authors.

References

Abizadeh, A. (2012). On the demos and its kin: Nationalism, democracy, and the boundary problem. *American Political Science Review, 106*, 867–882.
Barry, C., & Valentini, L. (2009). Egalitarian challenges to global egalitarianism: A critique. *Review of International Studies, 35*, 485–512.
Beitz, C. (2014). Internal and external. *Canadian Journal of Philosophy, 44*, 225–238.
Besson, S., & Martí, J. L. (in press). Legitimate actors of international law-making: Toward a theory of international democratic representation. *Jurisprudence*. doi:10.1080/20403313.2018.1442256
Bohman, J. (2007). *Democracy across borders*. Cambridge: MIT Press.
Braithwaite, J., & Drahos, P. (2000). *Global business regulation*. Cambridge: Cambridge University Press.

Buchanan, A. (2004). *Justice, legitimacy, and self-determination*. Oxford: Oxford University Press.
Buchanan, A. (2013). *The heart of human rights*. Oxford: Oxford University Press.
Buchanan, A., & Keohane, R. O. (2006). The legitimacy of global governance institutions. *Ethics & International Affairs, 20*, 405–437.
Christiano, T. (2015). Climate change and state consent. *Working Paper*. Retrieved September 20, 2017, from www.u.arizona.edu/~thomasc/Climate%20Change%20and%20State%20Consent.docx
Cohen, G. A. (2003). Facts and Principles. *Philosophy & Public Affairs, 31*, 211–245.
Cohen, G. A. (2009). *Why not socialism?* Princeton: Princeton University Press.
Dahl, R. A. (1999). Can international organizations be democratic? A skeptic's view. In I. Shapiro & C. Hacker-Cordon (Eds.), *Democracy's edges* (pp. 19–36). Cambridge: Cambridge University Press.
Dryzek, J. S. (2012). *Foundations and frontiers of deliberative governance*. Oxford: Oxford University Press.
Dryzek, J. S., & Niemeyer, S. (2008). Discursive representation. *American Political Science Review, 102*, 481–493.
Erman, E., & Möller, N. (2013). Three failed charges against ideal theory. *Social Theory & Practice, 39*(1), 19–44.
Erman, E, & Möller, N. (2018). *The practical turn in political theory*. Edinburgh: Edinburgh University Press.
Erman, E, & Möller, N. (2019). *A world of possibilities: the place of feasibility in political theory*. Res Publica (Online First).
Estlund, D. (2011). Human nature and the limits (If Any) of political philosophy. *Philosophy & Public Affairs, 39*, 207–237.
Estlund, D. (2014). Utopophobia. *Philosophy & Public Affairs, 42*, 113–134.
Farrelly, C. (2007). Justice in ideal theory: A refutation. *Political Studies, 55*, 844–864.
Gheaus, A. (2013). The feasibility constraint on the concept of justice. *The Philosophical Quarterly, 63*, 445–464.
Gilabert, P., & Lawford-Smith, H. (2012). Political feasibility: A conceptual exploration. *Political Studies, 60*, 809–825.
Grant, R. W., & Keohane, R. O. (2005). Accountability and abuses of power in world politics. *American Political Science Review, 99*, 29–43.
Green, J. F. (2013). *Rethinking private authority: agents and entrepreneurs in global environmental governance*. Princeton: Princeton University Press.
Hooghe, L., & Marks, G. (2015). Delegation and pooling in international organizations. *Review of International Organizations, 10*, 305–328.
Keohane, R. O., Macedo, S., & Moravcsik, A. (2009). Democracy-enhancing multilateralism. *International Organization, 63*, 1–31.
Lawford-Smith, Holly. (2013). Understanding political feasibility. *The Journal Of Political Philosophy, 21*, 243–259. doi:10.1111/jopp.2013.21.issue-3
Macdonald, T. (2008). *Global stakeholder democracy: Power and representation beyond liberal states*. Oxford: Oxford University Press.
Miller, D. (2010). Against Global Democracy. In K. Breen & S. O'Neill (Eds.), *After the nation: Critical reflections on post-nationalism* (pp. 141–160). Basingstoke: Palgrave.
Mills, C. (2005). 'Ideal Theory' as ideology. *Hypatia, 20*, 165–184.
Moravcsik, A. (2004). Is there a 'democratic deficit' in world politics? A framework for analysis. *Government and Opposition, 39*, 336–363.
Owen, D. (2012). Constituting the polity, constituting the demos. *Ethics & Global Politics, 5*, 129–152.

Räikkä, J. (1998). The feasibility condition in political theory. *The Journal of Political Philosophy, 6*, 27–40.

Rawls, J. (1999). *A theory of justice* (2nd ed.). Cambridge: Harvard University Press.

Ronzoni, M. (2009). The global order: A case of background injustice? A practice-dependent account. *Philosophy & Public Affairs, 37*, 229–256.

Sangiovanni, A. (2008). Justice and the priority of politics to morality. *The Journal of Political Philosophy, 16*, 137–164.

Schmidtz, D. (2011). Nonideal theory: What it is and what it needs to be. *Ethics, 121*, 772–796.

Scholte, J. A. (2014). Reinventing global democracy. *European Journal of International Relations, 20*, 3–28.

Sen, A. (2009). *The idea of justice*. Cambridge: Harvard University Press.

Simmons, J. (2010). Ideal and nonideal theory. *Philosophy & Public Affairs, 38*, 5–36.

Southwood, N. (2016). Does 'ought' imply 'feasible'? *Philosophy & Public Affairs, 44*, 7–45.

Southwood, N., & Wiens, D. (2016). Actual' does not imply 'feasible. *Philosophical Studies, 173*, 3037–3060.

Steffek, J. (2013). Explaining cooperation between IGOs and NGOs–push factors, pull factors, and the policy cycle. *Review of International Studies, 39*, 993–1013.

Tallberg, J., Sommerer, T., & Squatrito, T. (2016). Democratic memberships in international organizations: sources of institutional design. *The Review of International Organizations, 11*, 59–87.

Tallberg, J., Sommerer, T., Squatrito, T., & Jönsson, C. (2013). *The opening up of international organizations*. Cambridge: Cambridge University Press.

Ulaş, L. (2016). Doing things by halves: On intermediary global institutional proposals. *Ethics & Global Politics, 9*, 30223.

Valentini, L. (2012). Ideal vs. non-ideal theory: A conceptual map. *Philosophy Compass, 7*, 654–664.

Valentini, L. (2014). No global demos, no global democracy? A systematization and critique. *Perspectives on Politics, 20*, 789–807.

Wiens, D. (2015). Political ideals and the feasibility frontier. *Economics and Philosophy, 31*, 447–477.

The international rule of law

Carmen E. Pavel

ABSTRACT
The rule of law is a moral ideal that protects distinctive legal values such as generality, equality before the law, the independence of courts, and due process rights. I argue that one of the main goals of an international rule of the law is the protection of individual and state autonomy from the arbitrary interference of international institutions, and that the best way to codify this protection is through constitutional rules restraining the reach of international law into the internal affairs of a state. State autonomy does not have any intrinsic value or moral status of its own. Its value is derivative, resulting from the role it plays as the most efficient means of protecting autonomy for individuals and groups. Therefore, the goal of protecting state autonomy form the encroachment of international law will have to be constrained by, and balanced against the more fundamental goal of an international rule of law, the protection of the autonomy of individual persons, best realized through the entrenchment of basic human rights.

The fight for an international Rule of Law is a fight against politics, understood as a matter of furthering subjective desires, passions, prejudices and leading into an international anarchy. Though some measure of politics is inevitable (as we commonly assume), it should be constrained by non-political rules.

M Koskenniemi, *The Politics of International Law* (2011, p. 36).

The rule of law is a moral idea, if we understand the word 'moral' as implying limits on the means by which governments as well as persons pursue their goals. Theories of law that ignore this moral element cannot distinguish law as a constraint on the exercise of power from law as an instrument of power.

T. Nardin, '*Theorizing the International Rule of Law*' (2008, p. 385).

Introduction

International politics as the realm of lawless anarchy has long been superseded by law-governed interaction among states. International law reaches deeply into our ordinary lives, with rules regulating everything from trade in agricultural products, textiles and services, to air transport, pollution, the exploitation of ocean resources, and scientific research. Moreover, it is sufficiently institutionalized to contain agents which make, interpret, apply, and enforce rules. The expansion of international law brings with it the possibility of arbitrary interference with the authority of states and the rights of individuals. Organizations such the Security Council can authorize the use of coercive measures and even deadly force against any country, without accountability or the possibility for review of its decisions. Imposing some restrictions in the form of rule of law constraints, which require that international law officials are limited in their exercise of power, is desirable even for a young, incomplete system like international law.

Examples of overreach or arbitrary power exercised by international organizations are not difficult to find. In the early 2000s, the Security Council (SC) adopted sanctions under chapter VII of the UN Charter against individuals and entities who allegedly supported Al-Qaida and the Taliban. SC created a committee in charge of maintaining lists of individuals and organizations believed to aid and abet the terrorist network. It required all countries, including the European Union, to freeze the assets of those listed. In 2001, the SC committee added to the list Yassin Abdullah Kadi, a Saudi Arabia national and Swedish resident, and Al Barakaat, a Swedish charity for Somali refugees. Kadi and Al Barakaat brought suit against the EU for measures adopted in compliance with the sanctions, arguing that the measures violated their rights to property and due process. In a 2008 decision, the European Court of Justice ruled in favor of the complainants, explaining that the SC provided no avenues to access the justification for including particular names on the list, thereby denying the persons and organizations listed the possibility of challenging the measures taken against them. This constituted a violation of due process. Additionally, the court found that freezing financial and material assets without justification is an infringement of their rights to property. The judgment in Kadi is significant because it marks the first time a regional or national court argued that measures taken in compliance with SC sanctions violate fundamental rights (Kadi and Al Barakaat International Foundation v Council and Commission, 2008; Zgonec-Rozej, 2008). Although in Europe the application of the SC-sanctioned measures has been pushed back, they remain in force in much of the world.

As this example illustrates, given the extensive role it plays in regulating affairs among states, the potential for misuse or abuse of the authority of international law, and of inequities in the promulgation, interpretation, and application of its rules is vast. An international rule of law must constrain the arbitrary power of public officials, impose discipline on the requirements about the formal qualities of the law, such as publicity, prospectivity, and coherence, and protect the basic rights of its subjects. My purpose is to persuade skeptics that the moral ideal of the rule of law has a place in international politics and to offer an analysis of its implications for international law.

Yet there is an important sense in which it is premature to talk about an international rule of law. Most of the rules of international law are only binding on countries which have signed the treaties that gave rise to them, there are no courts with compulsory jurisdiction, and the rules are openly flouted when they become costly or run counter to state interest. The consensual character of international law, which means that states are only bound with their consent, makes it more akin to a network of contracts between private entities than to the legal system of developed liberal democracies. Talk of a rule of law for the international realm cannot target law in the usual sense of the term, as a system of general, universally binding requirements, administered by an institutional system characterized by clear hierarchies and equal access to courts for the peaceful and fair settlement of disputes.

This paper contributes a new perspective to the already extensive literature on an international rule of law, which is divided on the point or possibility of an international rule of law that mimics to the extent possible the features of a domestic rule of law (Besson, 2011; Hurd, 2015; McCorquodale, 2016; Waldron, 2006, 2011). There is wide agreement that the decentralized and consensual nature of international law, and the paucity of dispute resolution forums and of administrative and enforcement organs means that domestic rule of law requirements cannot be simply transplanted to the international realm. For example, it is not immediately clear who are the public officials of international law whose arbitrary power must be restrained. The requirements of an international rule of law must be interpreted and specified for the very different context of international law. I argue that one of the main goals of an international rule of the law is the protection of individual and state autonomy from the arbitrary interference of international institutions and that the best way to codify this protection is through constitutional rules restraining the reach of international law into the internal affairs of a state. State autonomy does not have any intrinsic value or moral status of its own. Its value is derivative, resulting from the role it plays as the most efficient means of protecting autonomy for individuals and groups. Therefore, the goal of protecting state autonomy form the encroachment of international law will have to be constrained by, and balanced against the more fundamental goal of an international rule of law, the protection of the autonomy of individual persons, best realized through the entrenchment of basic human rights.

The argument proceeds in several steps. I first provide an overview of different conceptions of rule of law, distinguishing between 'rule of law' and 'rule by law,' and between thin and thick conceptions. Some of the most defensible strands of rule of law theorizing share the notion that the rule of law demands restraint on arbitrary uses of power and serves an instrument for the protection of the equality and autonomy of the law's subjects. In this section I argue that thin or formal conceptions of the rule of law are incomplete, because they do not provide adequate constraints on legal systems to achieve equal protection under the law, and the protection of autonomy of the law's subjects . I then discuss the implications of a thick rule of law ideal for international law, arguing that conceptions of international rule of law that portray it as an instrument for the exercise of state power as opposed to a constraint on the public uses of power are not defensible. I then explain why it is important that international law protects the equality and autonomy of both states and of individuals. I conclude with reflections on the institutional requirements of the rule of law in international law.

The implications of this argument for the legitimacy of international law ought to be clear. States often question the authority of international law on the grounds of actual or potential arbitrary interference with their sovereign authority, the unequal application of the rules, the lack of coherence between the rules of different areas of international law, and uneven access to courts for the peaceful resolutions of disputes. The state-centric bias of international law means that individuals do not enjoy an adequate protection of their interests and often lack legal standing to demand accountability for the abuses that states inflict on them. Strengthening the rule of law could go a long way towards enhancing the normative legitimacy of international law, by giving states, individuals, and other agents better reasons to comply with its demands.

The point of the rule of law. Thin and thick conceptions

Unlike other concepts such as liberty, equality, democracy, whose value is regularly contested, the ideal of the rule of law receives near universal endorsement (Tamanaha, 2004; Trebilcock & Daniels, 2009). Closely associated with resistance to tyrannical government, protection of individual rights, and equality before the law, the idea of the rule of law took a historical hold in western absolutist monarchical states at the dawn of the Middle Ages, and played an important role in their gradual transition to fully fledged liberal democracies (Tamanaha, 2004, pp. 15–32).

Rule of law captures what are commonly described as formal and substantive features of the law. Among the formal features, the most important are 1. generality, 2. publicity, 3. prospectivity, 4. stability, 5. capacity to reflect clear, reasonable, and mutually consistent demands on individuals, 6. proportional punishment, 7. easy access to courts and 8. an independent judiciary. Formal features refer to the form and manner in which the law is promulgated rather than its content (Craig, 1997, p. 467). These features require, respectively: 1. That laws must not single out groups or individuals, but rather be addressed to all, and ensure that no one is above the law, especially public officials; 2. That the obligations that the law imposes are announced publicly, so that its subjects have reasonable notice of its demands and the opportunity to comply with them; 3. That laws are not retroactive, which would impede their ability to guide behavior; 4. That they are not changed too often, 5. That their demands cohere and they do not ask the impossible; 6. That violations do not incur draconian, disproportionate punishments; 7. That resort to justice is accessible to those who have been wronged through a court system designed to facilitate speedy and equitable resolution of complaints, and 8. That justice is administered by officials free from political control.

Among rule of law scholars there is wide agreement that the rule of law embodies a moral ideal: it requires constraints on the arbitrary and tyrannical use of government authority for the sake of protecting individual equality and autonomy (Fuller, 1969, p. 39; Hayek, 1978; Hart, 1984; Craig, 1997; Dworkin, 1998; Waldron, 2006; Raz, 2009, pp. 210–33). Law itself must embody a moral relationship among the law's subjects, which means that no one person is exempt from the law, or can exercise arbitrary will over another. Moreover, law's coercive capacity means that it must be applied with restraint, such that it does not unduly interfere with the subjects' life plans, and that it gives them opportunities to demand the accurate and equitable interpretation and application of the law and challenge its violation. The rule of law ideal embodies both a horizontal relationship of equality among the law's subjects, such that no one subject has more power or authority over others, and a vertical relationship between officials and subjects, such that officials are constrained to respect the autonomy of the subjects. This is why the protection of individual rights is an essential feature of many accounts of the rule of law in addition to the 'formal' features.

A first important distinction legal scholars and practitioners make is between 'rule of law' and 'rule by law.' Brian Tamanaha thoughtfully points out that rule by law, or simply legality, sometimes masquerades as the rule of law. For example, China is happy to pay lip service to the ideals of the latter while avoiding many of its essential constraints (Tamanaha, 2004, p. 92). 'Rule by law' or *legality* describes government action guided by law as opposed to the personal whims or arbitrary will of public officials. Yet the content of the rules can be such that they authorize the government to unduly limit people's independence, to create and cement inequality between the law's subjects, and to immunize public officials against rules that apply to ordinary citizens, and against challenges to their authority. Rule *by* law is not rule *of* law, because it need not impose constraints on government power other than the requirement to remain within the bounds of the law. Rule by law can move a legal system away from the rule of law rather than closer to it.[1]

One of the main reasons China has rule by law but not rule of law, is because it displays 'rule of law' features imperfectly or not at all (Chin, 2014). Any country like China that has general laws promulgated via a parliamentary and other law-making process, which guide both government and citizens' behavior, whatever their content, can display some measure of generality, publicity, prospectivity, stability, and consistency. But generality requires that public officials are not above the law, which is plainly not the case in China. One of the major problems of the Chinese legal system is the fact that, due to the continued control of the courts by the ruling communist party, party officials are not accountable to general applicable laws.[2] Legal professionals are routinely harassed, arrested, and tortured as a way to discourage challenges against government's authority (Pils 2017, p. 258; Haas, 2017). Furthermore, the commitment to proportional punishment, equal access to courts, or fidelity to constitutional rules is at the best uneven and at worst inexistent. For example, the constitution is vague, full of political slogans, and there is no provision for its enforcement, perhaps by design (Zhang, 2012, p. 65). Rule by law does very little to restrain abusive government practices, especially when the content of the law is oppressive or the law is applied without respect for due process: conviction rates in criminal trials near 100%, and are often based on coerced confessions. In the latest Rule of Law Index (2016), a ranking that measures restrictions on government power, the protection of fundamental right, civil and criminal justice, China ranked 80 out of 113 countries, and limited progress in the past few decades on the rule of law front goes hand in hand with backtracking due to an increase in abusive legal practices (Chin, 2016).[3]

As China's case illustrates, rule by law does not go very far in the direction of securing even the 'formal' features of the rule of law. Moreover, the language of 'formal' and 'substantive' obscures rather than illuminates the features of the rule of law, since it gives the wrong impression that formal features are value free or value neutral. Some of the so called 'formal' features protect substantive values. The idea that no one is above the law, especially public officials, is a clear expression of a commitment to the moral equality of individuals. The idea of proportional punishment likewise embodies the idea of retributive fairness, which serves a more abstract notion of justice as giving people their due. The language of thick and thin conceptions of the rule of law better captures the idea that 'formal' and 'substantive' criteria are part of a continuum of rule of law features imbued with moral commitments.

Thick conceptions of the rule of law include requirements about the content of the law, not just their formal features. A list of basic individual rights is often considered a necessary requirement of the rule of law ideal, such as the right to life and to physical integrity, rights of due process, rights to freedom of action and freedom of thought, and of private property. There are in fact two types of disagreements related to the substantive account of the rule of law: whether such an account is defensible and if so, which rights are worth including. I do not have the space to fully defend the idea that individual rights should be part of an account of the rule of law, but a few reasons in its favor are worth mentioning. The first thing to say in defense of incorporating rights protection is that what is considered as merely 'formal' rule of law is compatible with extensive tyranny. The 'formal' requirements about generality, stability, and even equality before law will be incompletely realized and will offer limited protection against abusive government policies. The limited formalism achieved under Chinese law shows that rule by law is compatible with predatory laws leading to widespread expropriation, or laws whose role is to oppress and intimidate. Formal restraints are an important first step in constraining the government's use of arbitrary power, but insufficient unless complemented by substantive constraints as well.

Second, it is hard to make sense of features such as equality before the law without individual rights protection. The point of insisting on equality before the law is to embody the fundamental notion that individuals are of equal moral worth, and the most secure embodiment of this notion is through the guarantee of rights protection. The point of the rule of law in limiting the exercise of political authority is to prevent regular abuses committed by governments against their citizens such as unjust imprisonment, torture, freedom from violence, large scale oppression of political dissenters or minorities, and these are rightly seen as violations of individuals and groups' fundamental rights. Rights violations are the reason government tyranny is seen as a universal bad and the reason for endorsing the moral value of the rule of law (Bennett, 2011, p. 613).

But if individual rights are to be part of rule of law requirements, which ones ought to be included? Proposals range from basic rights – Friedrich A. Hayek's suggestion to include the 'inalienable, individual right of man' can be read this way – to Ronald Dworkin's full set of social and political rights (Hayek, 2007, p. 63; Dworkin, 1985, pp. 11–12). The inclusion of all desirable political, social, and economic rights presents a serious problem, identified early on by Joseph Raz and H.L.A. Hart, namely that the more inclusive the concept of the rule of law becomes, the less it is distinguishable from other ideas such as justice or human rights, and the less it can be used as a concept that refers to the morality of law as distinguished from other normative concepts (Craig, 1997, pp. 468–69). This is precisely the ground on which Raz and Hart have objected to any thick/substantive rule of law ideal. They claim that 1. Including substantive moral values such as individual rights require a complete political philosophy, and 2. It would render the concept of the rule of law indistinguishable from other useful normative concepts such as democracy, human rights, or justice, and thus it would cease to serve its distinctive social function of providing a normative standard for evaluating legal systems.

We can reply to those like Raz and Hart that defend a thin/formal rule of law that the distinction between formal and substantive criteria is somewhat strained as 'formal' rule of law is based on substantive values such as equality, autonomy, fairness, justice. As I noted above, many of the so called 'formal' features of the rule of law are grounded in moral commitments. Justice in the legal context is best understood not as the most encompassing political and social value, but as the demand that the law embodies reasonable behavioral standards that are attached to proportional sanctions, fairness in the administration of the law, and equality of treatment before the law coupled with proper respect for and effective protection of basic rights. These are all contestable moral commitments, and supposing that focusing on the formal features of the rule of law avoids them misunderstands the rationale for having formal features of rule of law at all. The claim against Raz and Hart is not that 'formal' rule of law is no improvement over arbitrary uses of the law, but that the grounds on which to distinguish formal from substantive conceptions of the rule of law is weak, if it merely relies on the fact that formal rule of law avoids substantive ethical commitments. It does not.

The second concern is harder to dismiss, as turning the rule of law into the Trojan horse of all of the values we care about risks indeed making the concept indistinguishable from other substantive normative commitments that we resort to in order to pass judgments of justice and legitimacy. Raz and Hart are right that going the Dworkinian path takes us away from the rule of law understood as a moral ideal embodied in the law and closer toward a fully-fledged theory of justice. One way to avoid this trap is to pack a minimal account of individual rights into the concept of the rule of law. For less than the full panoply of rights, the choice of what to include will be somewhat open-ended, but at a minimum, it would have to count among its protections the security of persons and property, due process rights, and rights to freedom of action and expression. The open-ended nature of the basic rights necessary for a defensible account of the rule of law is an advantage as it enhances the possibility to specify those right through a political process where different states and groups negotiate and compromise, which will make them more likely to be accepted and implemented, and not through philosophical armchair theorizing. Nonetheless, if the more defensible conception of the rule of law is one that includes the protection of basic individual rights, what follows for the structure and practice of international law? The next sections are devoting to answering this question.

Do we need an international rule of law?

Ian Hurd maintains that the domestic ideal of the rule of law cannot capture how international law works in practice. The international rule of law simply reflects the way in which state use law to justify and pursue foreign policy (Hurd, 2015, p. 367). The concepts of domestic and international rule of law arose in response to different problems. The point of domestic rule of law is to place limits on the exercise of centralized power and to protect the equality of citizens, while the point of the international rule of law is to respond to the lack of a centralized international authority and to cement the consensual character of law among states (Hurd, 2015, pp. 366–367).

For Hurd, both the purposes and the institutional requirements of the international rule of law must be different from those of the domestic rule of law: international law regulates relations among states, while domestic law regulates relations among individuals and other non-state agents. The implication of this difference for Hurd is that the international rule of law must affirm the instrumental role international law plays in serving state interests. Each state has a different constellation of obligations, and states will use international law to justify and legitimate their actions. He claims that 'in the interstate setting, this goal of a unified set of public rules that applies to all subjects cannot be achieved or even approximated because states retain the authority to accept, reject, or modify their legal obligations through treaty accession, reservations, and persistent objections' (Hurd, 2015, p. 382). Therefore, the universally biding character of domestic law cannot be a feature of international law, and therefore many of the characteristics of the domestic rule of law that come with it, such as equality before the law, must be abandoned.

Hurd makes a good case that the steady and large amount of formalization of the relations between states through treaties constitutes a big step in the direction of rule-governed interaction, as opposed to leaving them to the vagaries of politics, power imbalances, and prejudice (Hurd, 2015, p. 378). Codification brings with it the important formal features of the rule of law such as clarity, predictability, prospectivity, coherence, and creates the basic rules that structure the relations among states. The international order is 'constitutional' in Hurd's view, in the sense that it generates rules that explain how states can make treaties and the ways in which those treaties create responsibilities for them. But it is not 'constitutional' in the more traditional sense in which it protects certain fundamental rights of the law's subject against encroachment by its institutions.

Hurd's position is deeply problematic if an international rule of law is understood simply as a vehicle for facilitating the realization of state interests. Hurd is right that the different structure and purposes of international law means that its institutional requirements must be different. But he is wrong to equate the rule of international law with legality, or 'rule by law.' First of all, his approach fails to take the rule of law seriously as a moral ideal whose primary function is to place constraints on the exercise of power by subjects against one another and by political authority against subjects. As

Terry Nardin aptly observes, this position belongs to a class of international relations views that fail to distinguish law as an instrument of power from law as a constraint on power (2008, p. 385). Hurd is repeating the common refrain among international relations scholars that since the circumstances of international anarchy make it impossible to realize uniform, enforceable law among states, international law must be by necessity an instrument of state foreign policy rather than a common instrument for solving public goods problems, or for achieving peace and justice. There is no distinction on this view between law and mere power.

Law is not only distinct from power but it must be the antithesis of power if it is to serve its social purpose properly. Law must constrain the power that individuals exercise over one another for the sake of peaceful coexistence, it must recognize and protect their equal moral status, and it must assist them in the pursuit of individual and common ends, including public goods. And above all, law must constrain the exercise of power by the public officials. The ideal rule of law is one of the ways in which law instantiates these values. While it is perfectly possible to have law as a set of primary rules that direct subjects about appropriate standards of behavior which lacks many of these features, no system of law is merely instrumental, and serves solely for the purpose of realizing affirming the power and interests of its subjects. Mere instrumentality is actually impossible to realize, since the law's subjects exercise their power in conflicting ways that threaten each other's survival and limit the pursuit of each other's interests. International law cannot be merely an instrument of state power simply because different states may wish to pursue mutually exclusive ends, and the role of international law is to limit the ways in which states can harm each other and their citizens in pursuit of these ends, while protecting a sphere of autonomous action for states and individuals.

International law has distinctive substantive and structural features ill-suited at least for now for some of the common ways to implement the domestic rule of law. The strong consensual element of international law means that states are for the most part only bound by treaties and rules they explicitly agree to. The implication of this feature is that very few international rules, with the exception of the UN Charter, customary law, and the decisions of the Security Council bind everyone. This means that equality before law is limited under treaty law to states that accede to a particular treaty.[4] For example, treaties protecting various human rights bind only the states that have ratified them, and the statute creating the International Criminal Court binds only the states that have become members of the court.

This makes the character of international law different from domestic law where law binds individuals with or without their consent. While domestic law can also distinguish between subjects based on consent, say due to the law of contract, it typically contains a large number of legal rules which apply regardless of subjects' consent, including those restricting the use of violence, granting due process rights, or subjecting public officials to generally applicable law, and thus equality before the law means that individual are subjected to laws with general applicability, and that they possess equal rights and obligations. By contrast, states' obligations vary with their willingness to commit to certain rules and not others, and there is no minimally required set of rules set are obligated to follow, outside of the meager constraints on the use of force and the principle of sovereign equality set out in the UN Charter. A well-known point of contention is that the authority of the International Criminal Court only applies to states that have ratified the Rome Statute, which means that states are divided between those whose officials and citizens are bound by rules for criminal accountability and those to whom they do not.

Equality before the law is necessary even in a legal system such as international law, because under a consent-based system, powerful states often manage to extricate themselves from their obligations to respect even the least intrusive general rules, such as non-interference with the sovereign prerogatives of other states, and from rules that should have a more general character, such as the international rules for criminal accountability. Consent cannot be determinative of states' rights and obligations in a world in which political officials often misrepresent their citizens' interests by withholding consent from rules that could better protect these interests, at least in the case of non-democratic/authoritarian states. The normative significance of state consent is weakened by its ability to divide the world into those to whom the rules apply and those to whom it does not.

We should acknowledge with Hurd that legalization is an important step towards the implementation of the international rule of law. Nonetheless, it cannot constitute the endpoint of efforts to build the rule of law. An ideal of an international rule of law can inform efforts to reform the current system to reduce power asymmetries, and place guarantees in place to ensure a more even distribution of rights and responsibilities among states. Unless one believes that feasibility constraints for an international rule of law are so great that they disqualify it as a goal worth pursuing, we should consider possible avenues for reform in international law that place limits on the arbitrary use of power, defend the equality and autonomy of individuals, and bind public officials to generally recognized rules. It is difficult to contemplate at this point in time a world in which states have stronger and equal obligations under international law given that states have a propensity to guard their sovereign prerogative jealously. Yet the domestic rule of law developed as a response to similar circumstances, in which individuals and groups enjoyed unequal status and power, there was no unified system of rules that applied to all, and legal rules lacked generality, coherence, or fairness in their application.

The rule of law for domestic law was an achievement many centuries in the making, and it started from structural background conditions not very different than the ones present in international law today. Douglass North, John Joseph Wallis, and Barry Weingast argue that the formation of modern states can be best understood as evolving from 'natural state' political orders, characterized by legal compromises among the powerful, dominant individuals, who agreed to respect each other's privileges, including rights to territory and resources, and restrict their use of violence. 'Natural orders' were not inclusive, open, social orders because these privileges did not extend equally to the less powerful and more vulnerable members of the society in the same way that they do today in liberal democratic societies (North, Wallis, & Weingast, 2013, pp. 18–21, 30–76). States today rely on international law to protect their sovereign authority and territory, but at the same time insulate themselves from rules the more powerful they are, which leaves the less economically and militarily powerful states vulnerable to abuse. The former can withhold consent to international treaties that impose serious restrictions on their capacity to act, while the latter are limited in their capacity to use international law to limit violations of their rights and to protect their interests. Hierarchy, status, and raw power are as much characteristics of international law today as they are of natural orders that characterized early state formation.[5]

International law in its current form is a rule *by* law system in which the officials in the system are guided by rules in their interaction, rather than a rule *of* law system, in which the officials are both guided and restricted by rules, and the subjects enjoy equality before the law. Rule *by* law is not acceptable as the ultimate expression of the rule of law because it does not achieve the aims of the rule of law, which are protecting the autonomy of the subjects and restraining the arbitrary use of power. While some existing features of international law will make it difficult to move beyond a consensual 'rule by law' framework, these features could be changed gradually to move international law toward a stronger rule of law system. Setting up general rules, expanding the number and reach of courts that give both states and individuals access to impartial dispute settlement, and creating more effective systems of enforcement are achievable given the rapid legalization of international politics today.

Therefore, an approach that takes the international rule of law as a moral ideal seriously requires the strengthening of features that circumscribe the authority of public officials and protect individual and state autonomy. Of the eight 'formal' features 1. generality, 2. publicity, 3. prospectivity, 4. stability, 5. capacity to reflect clear, reasonable, and mutually consistent demands on individuals, 6. proportional punishment, 7. easy access to courts and 8. an independent judiciary, only 2. publicity, 3. prospectivity, 4, stability and to some extent 5. capacity to reflect clear, reasonable and mutually consistent demands on subjects, are realized in international law. The increasing legalization of the relations among states means that more of their interactions and disagreements are governed by rules laid out in advance, that are relatively clear, stable, and public. But generality is not yet a feature of international law, nor is easy access to courts, despite the rise in the number of international courts and tribunals. States are still the main subjects in international law, and they alone have standing to bring claims to most international courts. Furthermore, their legal standing has no effect when another state party to a dispute rejects the jurisdictional authority of an international court. Punishment for violations of international law is limited, which means proportional punishment is not yet a feature of rule-governed interaction among states. International law has been described as a self-help system and that description still applies today (Kelsen, 1952, p. 14).

The purpose of the international rule of law

In the absence of a bureaucratic structure that closely resembles a world government, two questions arise: 1. Which agents have the potential to exercise arbitrary power that must be limited? and 2. Who are the subjects of international law whose autonomy must be protected from arbitrary interference? The answer to the second question is more straightforward. International law is addressed mostly to states, with an increasing but still small role for individuals and other group and corporate agents – companies, indigenous groups, NGOs – as direct subjects of international law. An international rule of law would need to protect all of these agents, as well as any other actors that fall under its remit directly or indirectly through the mediating power of states, from arbitrary power exercised by global governance institutions and international officials in their exercise of their capacities.

The answer to the first question is that all of the agents that make, interpret, and apply international law can potentially exercise arbitrary power that must be limited. These are primarily states, who have the power to make treaties, and the international institutions that states endow with autonomous capacity to apply and enforce the rules, such as the International Court of Justice, the World Trade Organization, various ad-hoc tribunals and regional courts and organizations, and the agencies of the United Nations system, including the Security Council. Thus states have a dual agency both as subjects and officials of international law.

The idea that international law should be promulgated and constrained such that it protects state autonomy is very much in dispute. Jeremy

Waldron argues that the protection of state autonomy should not be one of the aims of an international rule of law (Waldron, 2006, p. 18). He draws an analogy with domestic law, for which he distinguishes two general subjects, individuals and administration, and argues that only individuals are entitled to the benefit of the rule of law and the protection of their autonomy. The rule of law creates a predictable environment in which individuals exercise their freedom and plan their life secure in the knowledge that no arbitrary use of state power will undo their plans at will. Administration, by which he means the collection of government bureaucratic bodies, holds no entitlement to the protection of its autonomy from the law in the same way. Whereas less law is better for individual autonomy, no such presumption is warranted with respect to administration. In fact, more law is required to regulate administrative bodies rather than less, because this means that more of their actions are taken in accordance with rules laid out in advance and that their discretion is limited accordingly (Waldron, 2006, pp. 18–19).

As officials in charge of making international law, states are in the same position as domestic administration, Waldron claims. Their behavior must be constrained and their discretion limited by more law not less, and they do not gain the presumption in favor of the protection of their autonomy. States are constituted as legal entities of international law and their autonomy does not rest on a fundamental normative principle in the same way that individual autonomy does in domestic law (Waldron, 2006, p. 23, 2011, p. 339).

But is it true that international law should not protect state autonomy? What would be the consequence of extensive regulatory intrusion of international law into member states, with no limit on the ability of international law to regulate or change national laws, and to create differential protections and privileges for different states such that the autonomy of some is protected but not of all? To some extent this is the current reality of international law, with the permanent members of the Security Council exercising disproportionate power over other states and enjoying some measure of immunity from the rules that these other states are subjected to. Indeed, as Anthony Anghie has argued, it is plausible to argue that the Security Council divides the world into two: those to whom the rules do not apply (the five permanent members), and those to whom they do.[6] Antoinette Scherz and Alain Zysset (this issue) argue that enhancing the normative legitimacy of the Security Council requires indeed reforming the membership structure, although any substantial reforms will meet with serious resistance. Nonetheless, without such reforms, the imbalance of power at the Security Council seriously affects the fairness and legitimacy of international law as a whole, and the practical consequence of this imbalance can be a significant loss to the value of democratic self-determination within states. It opens the possibility of such severe erosion of sovereignty and all of the values it protects (independence from others, local rule, diversity of political and institutional cultures) that it raises questions about the legitimacy of international law as a whole. The existing institutional set-up could end up denying states the liberty of pursuing diverse goals, and it would misdirect the power of international law in an oppressive, paternalistic direction (Nardin, 1983).

States are entitled to autonomy not for their own sake, but for the sake of the individuals they represent and govern. Thus, the value of state autonomy rests on the value of individual autonomy as a fundamental normative commitment, and in this sense, it is derivative. States' interest in autonomy is important because it protects individual and collective self-determination. As officials of international law, we can insist that states should be rule-bound in their law-making capacity. But as subjects of international law, states are entitled to a wide berth to make decisions in line with the collective wishes of their populations, and the fact that state autonomy is instrumentally valuable does not mean it carries little weight. Precisely because of its role in protecting individual autonomy, state autonomy under international law should enjoy the widest presumption. At the same time, states are not entitled to unlimited autonomy. State autonomy must be limited for the sake of other states' autonomy and the autonomy of individuals who are their own citizens or the citizens of other states. For example, international law cannot legitimate a state interfering in the autonomous decisions of other states, even if that interference has been justified via internal democratic processes. Limitations on state autonomy are justified in the name of severe violations of individual autonomy, of other states' autonomy, of solving cooperation problems such as public goods and collective action dilemmas, and in the interest of international peace and order.

Waldron quotes Abram Chayes approvingly to suggest that as mere officials of international law, states must be bound by law and are not entitled to respect for their autonomy: 'if states are the "subjects" of international law, they are so, not as private persons are the "subjects" of municipal legal systems, but as government bodies are the "subjects" of constitutional arrangements' (Waldron, 2011, p. 328). But this position does not follow from a proper description of states as both *subjects and officials* of international law. As law-makers, states are subject of international law as governmental bodies are subject of constitutional arrangements. But as addressees of the law, they must be granted wide protections for their autonomous law-making capacity internally.

States are not the only officials of international law. International law-making organizations, including international courts, must exercise their powers through laws that are prospective, general, stable, reflect demands that are reasonable and compatible with each other, whose operation is independent of political influence and can provide easy access for the law's subjects, whether states, individuals, or other agents operating in international politics.

State autonomy is valuable to the extent it protects individual autonomy. The protection of individual autonomy in international law can be realized through the protection of basic human rights, and through rules that prevent states and international organization from unduly interfering with the ability of individuals to exercise their freedom and plan their lives. This is in effect the primary goal of an international rule of law, compatible with understanding states as agents of their people and acting on their behalf. International law must protect individuals from their own states, other states or agents, and states from each other and from international institutions (Waldron, 2011, p. 324).

The institutional contours of the international rule of law

Both states and individuals enjoy some degree of rights protection in international law. States benefit from rights of non-interference with their sovereign authority, and limited rights of sovereign equality under the rules of the UN Charter, while individuals benefit from an extensive network of human rights treaties. But there are still many unresolved conflicts among the rights of states, and between the rights of states and those of individuals, as debates about the permissibility of humanitarian intervention or limits on sovereign immunity illustrate (Knuchel, 2010; Nardin and Williams 2005; Pattison, 2012).

Realizing the moral ideal of the rule of law in international law requires institutional reform. At the very minimum, we should move in the direction of creating a minimal set of universally binding rules and courts with compulsory jurisdiction, which guarantee better access to all of the subjects of international law to the resolution of grievances of the peaceful settlement of conflicts.

Many if not all of the institutions and courts operating in international law which contribute to making, interpreting, applying rules, and adjudicate conflicts, including the World Trade Organization, the International Criminal Court, the Law of the Sea Tribunal carry the potential to abuse their authority, and currently they face little oversight. Correcting this significant shortcoming of international law requires rules that specify in detail the limits of the authority delegated to international governance institutions, and empowers agents to check each other's arbitrary exercise of authority. Still, the international rule of law demands more than oversight and accountability ensured through institutional checks and balances. It demands that equality before law be strengthened and the protection of basic interests of the participant in the international order be made explicit through a list of rights and entitlements that receive special status as fundamental building blocks of an international legal order.

There are various institutional alternatives for building of these features of the international rule of law, but one that merits attention is a constitutional international order. A constitutional international order defines the division of authority between international institutions and states, prescribes rights of non-interference for states, and enumerates basic individual rights deserving special weight in the making, interpretation, and application of international law.

The way to solve the problem of state opt out of the morally required minimum of law is to create bodies whose authority is to create international law that applies universally, evenly, and efficiently. For example, giving the ICC jurisdiction over crimes committed by the citizens of all states, not just member states, would be a step forward in this direction. Indeed, as Thomas Christiano argues, it is hard to see the exclusion of some of the most powerful states from its jurisdiction as something other than a bold attempt to place themselves above international law (Christiano, this issue). States could adopt universally binding rules is via some form of constitutionalization, which would spell out some minimal, binding obligations and rights for states, individuals, and other subjects of international law. Constitutionalization can preserve a substantial level of autonomy for individual states. The point of a constitutional order is to make sure that it does precisely this.

Developing an account of the constitutionalization of international law goes beyond the aim of this paper. However, others have offered instructive insights. Christian Tomuschat describes an international constitution as 'a legal framework of limited number of basic rules' to constrain states, and 'which determines their basic rights and obligations with or without their will' (1993, p. 211). Judge James Crawford, who has served at the International Court of Justice, defends a constitutional order which involves constraints on state powers and on international institutions, and guarantees for rights (2014, pp. 455, 460–61, 466). He argues that the process of constitutionalization should build on the emerging hierarchy in international law, that places the UN Charter with its the restriction on the use of force of at its core, along with *jus cogens* norms and obligations *erga omnes* (Crawford, 2014, pp. 465–66).

While a global constitutional order would constitute a substantive, qualitative transformation of the relationship of national to international law, such transformation would not be wholesale. Global constitutionalism could still preserve the largely consensual nature of international law but make changes in the direction of creating universally binding law. This change will alter the relationship of states to international law on a number of crucial issues, and we can insist international law does so only for those issues to avoid overreach and the disabling of state sovereignty.

The road to an international constitutional order will be long and hard, fraught with resistance from states and international organizations alike, and punctuated by difficult choices about the precise content of the constitutional rules. But it marks one of the surest ways to ensure the strengthening of the international rule of law. Building the rule of international law enhances the legitimacy of international law by giving states and individual better reasons to comply with its demands. For example, global constitutional norms which limit the authority of international law, mandate or proscribe certain behaviors for all subjects, and create courts with universal compulsory jurisdiction, can stave off concerns with arbitrary interference with state sovereignty, the unequal application of the rules, and the lack of access to courts for the peaceful resolution of disputes. A global constitution can address all of the existing limitations of international law in this respect while protecting an important sphere of autonomous state action. And it can do so consistent with a fundamental commitment to respect the basic rights of individuals on behalf of whom states exercise their authority.

Notes

1. I thank Terry Nardin for this point.
2. For example, the party appoints key members of courts or is able to veto appointments (Peerenboom, 2002, p. 8).
3. The Rule of Law Index https://worldjusticeproject.org/our-work/wjp-rule-law-index/wjp-rule-law-index-2016 (accessed 24 September 2017) is a project of the non-profit World Justice Project, set up by the American Bar association with support from the International Bar Association and other groups.
4. Even under treaty law, state members of the same treaty do not have the same obligations. The practice of reservations allows states to opt out of certain provisions of a treaty. In customary international law, persistent objectors are states who explicitly and repeatedly claim an exemption from a generally accepted customary rule.
5. Consider also the United States during its westward expansion. New territories, although formally under the jurisdiction of federal law, had weak law, applied unevenly, with courts which were few and far between, under-resourced, and there was little if any supervision of legal officials. See (Kenyon, 1968, pp. 682–83). International law today shares many of these characteristics.
6. Anthony Anghie conference presentation, The Global Rule of Law, Singapore, February, 2017.

Acknowledgments

I wish to thank the two anonymous referees for their comments. I also thank Cord Schmelzle for the invitation to present this paper at the Justitia Amplificata conference 'Legitimacy Beyond the State: Normative and Conceptual Questions' in Bad Homburg in January 2017, as well as to all the participants for thoughtful questions and suggestions. Thanks are due to Patrick Taylor Smith for the invitation to present the paper to the 'Global Rule of Law' conference in Singapore in February 2017, and to Terry Nardin for his criticism and advice. The other participants in the conference inspired me with a great set of papers. Additionally, I have benefitted from feedback from the audience at the European Consortium for Political Research conference in Oslo, Norway in September 2017.

Disclosure statement

No potential conflict of interest was reported by the author.

References

Bennett, M. J. (2011). Hart and Raz on the non-instrumental moral value of the rule of law: A reconsideration. *Law and Philosophy*, *30*(5), 603–635.
Besson, S. (2011). Sovereignty, international law and democracy. *European Journal of International Law*, *22*(2), 373–387.
Chin, J. (2014, October 20). 'Rule of law' or 'rule by law'? In China, a preposition makes all the difference. *Wall Street Journal*. Retrieved from https://blogs.wsj.com/chinarealtime/2014/10/20/rule-of-law-or-rule-by-law-in-china-a-preposition-makes-all-the-difference/.
Chin, J. (2016, October 20). China lags behind in rule-of-law ranking. *Wall Street Journal*. Retrieved from https://blogs.wsj.com/chinarealtime/2016/10/20/china-lags-behind-in-rule-of-law-ranking/.
Craig, P. P. (1997). Formal and substantive conceptions of the rule of law: An analytical framework. *Public Law*, 21, 467–487.
Crawford, J. (2014). *Chance, order, change: The course of international law, general course on public international law*. Leiden: Brill-Nijhoff.
Dworkin, R. (1985). *A matter of principle* (Reprint ed.). Cambridge: Harvard University Press.
Dworkin, R. (1998). *Law's Empire* (New ed.). Oxford: Hart Publishing.
Fuller, L. L. (1969). *The morality of law: Revised* (Revised ed.). New Haven: Yale University Press.
Haas, B. (2017, January 24). China abandoning rule of law, human rights lawyers say. *The Guardian*. Retrieved from https://www.theguardian.com/world/2017/jan/24/china-abandoning-rule-of-law-human-rights-lawyers-say.
Hart, H. L. A. (1984). *Essays in jurisprudence and philosophy*. Oxford: Oxford University Press.

Hayek, F. A. (1978). *Law, legislation and liberty, volume 1: Rules and order*. Chicago: University Of Chicago Press.
Hayek, F. A. (2007). *The road to serfdom: Text and documents–the definitive edition (The collected works of F.A. Hayek)*. Chicago: University Of Chicago Press.
Hurd, I. (2015). The international rule of law and the domestic analogy. *Global Constitutionalism*, 4(3), 365–395.
Kelsen, H. (1952). *Principles of international law*. New York: Rinehart & Co.
Kenyon, C. (1968). Legal lore of the wild west: A bibliographical essay. *California Law Review*, 56(3), 681.
Knuchel, S. (2010). State immunity and the promise of Jus Cogens. *Northwestern University Journal of International Human Rights*, 9, 149.
Koskenniemi, M. (2011). *Politics of international law*. Oxford: Bloomsbury Publishing.
McCorquodale, R. (2016). Defining the international rule of law: Defying gravity? *International & Comparative Law Quarterly*, 65(2), 277–304.
Nardin, T. (1983). *Law, morality, and the relations of states*. Princeton: Princeton University Press.
Nardin, T. (2008). Theorising the international rule of law. *Review of International Studies*, 34(3), 385–401.
Nardin, T., & Melissa, W. (2005). *Humanitarian intervention: NOMOS XLVII*. New York: NYU Press.
North, D. C., Wallis, J. J., & Weingast, B. R. (2013). *Violence and social orders: A conceptual framework for interpreting recorded human history*. New York: Cambridge University Press.
Pattison, J. (2012). *Humanitarian intervention and the responsibility to protect: Who should intervene?* Oxford: Oxford University Press.
Peerenboom, R. (2002). *China's long march toward rule of law*. Cambridge: Cambridge University Press.
Pils, E. (2017). The party and the law. In Willy Wo-Lap Lam (Ed.), *Routledge handbook of the Chinese communist party* (pp. 248–265). Abingdon: Routledge.
Raz, J. (2009). *The authority of law: Essays on law and morality* (2nd ed.). Oxford: Oxford University Press.
Tamanaha, B. Z. (2004). *On the rule of law: History, politics, theory*. Cambridge: Cambridge University Press.
Tomuschat, C. (1993). Obligations arising for states without or against their will. *Recueil Des Cours*, 241, 195–374.
Trebilcock, M. J., & Daniels, R. J. (2009). *Rule of law reform and development: Charting the fragile path of progress*. Cheltenham: Edward Elgar.
Waldron, J. (2006). The rule of international law. *Harvard Journal of Law and Public Policy*, 30(1), 15–30.
Waldron, J. (2011). Are sovereigns entitled to the benefit of the international rule of law? *European Journal of International Law*, 22(2), 315–343.
Yassin Abdullah Kadi and Al Barakaat International Foundation v Council and Commission. (2008). *European court of justice*.
Zgonec-Rozej, M. 2008. Kadi & Al Barakaat v. Council of the EU & EC Commission: European Court of Justice Quashes a Council of the EU Regulation Implementing UN Security Council Resolutions. *ASIL Insights*, 12(22). Retrieved from https://www.asil.org/insights/volume/12/issue/22/kadi-al-barakaat-v-council-eu-ec-commission-european-court-justice.
Zhang, Q. (2012). *The constitution of China: A contextual analysis*. Oxford: Hart Publishing.

The arbitrary circumscription of the jurisdiction of the international criminal court

Thomas Christiano

ABSTRACT
As it is currently legally constituted, the International Criminal Court has no jurisdiction over the world's most important military powers – United States, China and Russia-for the most serious crimes that can be committed in the international system (unless their members commit the crimes on the territory of a state that has ratified the ICC). It is hard to see the restricted jurisdiction of the International Criminal Court as anything other than the bald placing of the most powerful members of the international political community above the law while the rest of the community remains subject to it. At the same time, one essential element of the legitimacy of the International Criminal Court is that it is founded on state consent. But this does not get the International Criminal Court entirely off the hook. I will argue that the circumscription of the jurisdiction of the court is arbitrary and in violation of fundamental norms of justice and that this threatens the legitimacy of the Court. We are facing a legitimacy dilemma between the need for state participation in the creation of international law and the requirements of the rule of law.

Introduction

As it is currently legally constituted, the International Criminal Court has no jurisdiction over the world's most important military powers for the most serious crimes that can be committed in the international system (unless their members commit the crimes on the territory of a state that has ratified the ICC). The crimes of genocide, war crimes, crimes against humanity and the crime of aggression are acknowledged by all to be the most serious. The United States, China and Russia have not ratified the Rome Statute and they are each permanent members of the Security Council and so can veto any attempt by the Security Council to refer their nationals to the Court. These powers do not belong to any other system for prosecuting serious international crimes and they have shown no appetite for investigating their nationals who may be high-level perpetrators of these crimes. They seem to be benefited from a regime of impunity when it comes to their own possible violations of the most serious crimes. At the same time, these states are very much a part of the nascent international political community. They are the dominant elements in the Security Council. They have referred cases to the Court for investigation. They assist the court in its investigative activities. And they are clearly interested parties with regard to the investigations of these crimes since they are routinely engaged in military and economic activities around the world.

It is hard to see this restricted jurisdiction as anything other than the bald placing of the most powerful members of the international political community above the law while the rest of the community remains subject to it. This along with the reality of selective prosecution of cases that have so far excluded the powerful states and their friends from serious investigation suggests an international criminal justice system that violates one of the most fundamental norms of equality before the law that is accepted as a principle of criminal justice everywhere. It calls into question the legitimacy of the international criminal justice system and the International Criminal Court insofar as it plays a residual role in this system.

At the same time, one essential element of the legitimacy of the International Criminal Court is that it is founded on state consent. The requirement of state consent carries with it the circumscription of jurisdiction to crimes committed by nationals of the ratifying states or committed on the territory of these states (though, importantly, it is not the basis of jurisdiction concerning cases referred to it by the Security Council). I will argue that the need for state consent is a defensible part of the current international political system; it is the main means by which international institutions and law are accountable to societies and the people who make them up. But this does not get the International Criminal Court entirely off the hook. I will argue that the circumscription of the jurisdiction of the court is arbitrary and in violation of fundamental norms of justice and that this threatens the legitimacy of the Court. We are facing a legitimacy dilemma between the need for state participation in the creation of international law and the requirements of the rule of law.

In this paper, I vindicate the idea that the jurisdiction of the International Criminal Court is arbitrarily circumscribed and that this does damage to its legitimacy. I start by articulating some basic aspects of the legitimacy of an international court. I then articulate the nature of the problem of the arbitrary circumscription of jurisdiction. I develop a conception of the international political system and the role of state consent as well as the mandatory aims of protection of persons against serious human rights violations. I argue that the non-consent of major powers to the Rome Statute does not defeat the charge that the ICC's jurisdiction is arbitrarily circumscribed. I elaborate two problems of legitimacy the circumscription of the court's jurisdiction implies. I discuss some objections and some qualifications to my reasoning before I conclude.

Legitimacy and the international criminal court

What does legitimacy in the International Criminal Court consist of? The court investigates, tries, convicts (or acquits) and sentences persons for crimes against humanity, war crimes, genocide and the crime of aggression (Rome Statute, Article 5). The ICC is authorized to investigate cases without interference. The court has the power to determine whether a situation is worth investigating. If it decides that it is, it may summon witnesses, issue indictments, make requests for evidence and issue arrest warrants. It establishes a trial and thereby can decide guilt and innocence and decide an appropriate sentence, thus imposing punishment. I deal with the actions of the Court as all of a piece since the jurisdictional issues arise for each and all of the actions of the Court.

Legitimacy, as I understand it here, involves the moral power of some institutionally defined agent to impose duties and other reasons for action on other agents (Raz, 1986, chap 3; Simmons, 2000). The exercise of this moral power has the consequence that persons or groups have content-independent reasons to act as the institution directs even when they disagree with the judgment of the power exercising agent. The problem to which moral legitimacy judgments provide the answer is to give a morally satisfactory resolution to the issue of who decides and how the decision is to be made when there is substantial disagreement on the issues relevant to the decision. A criminal court decides on questions of guilt and innocence and proper punishment; and when it has great legitimacy, even those who disagree with the verdict, the sentence or even the indictment, have duties to comply with the directives of the court. It is important to the legitimacy of the ICC that it decides guilt and innocence regardless of the political processes of the political society in which the crimes are committed. This is explicitly correlated with the legal duties of States, their officials and non-state actors that have the political power to arrest the persons, cooperate with the investigation, and enforce the judgments of the court (Rome Statute, Articles 86, 89 and 93).

Once the ICC enters into a conflict zone and indicts someone, an arrest warrant must be served even if there is a process establishing amnesty of one form or another. This means that fundamental tools for the resolution of political conflict are mitigated. The political participants have duties to arrest the indicted party. This is one of the things, in addition to the fact that it orders the deprivation of liberty of persons, that makes the ICC and its prosecutorial arm so contentious.

There are three basic dimensions of the legitimacy of a court. First, the court and the law it applies must be properly established by a political society in whose name the court acts. This dimension has both substantive and legal aspects. Is the law the court applies just? Are the processes by which the court is established genuinely fair? Second, the court must faithfully apply the law of that political society. Third, the court must apply that law effectively and impartially to the members of the society in a way that observes due process of law. Let us call these the *political*, the *legality* and the *impartiality* conditions of legitimacy for courts.

The ICC is meant to be legitimate on these three dimensions. Thus, it is established by means of a treaty by members of the international community, which, I will argue, is a distinctive type of political society. It applies the law of the political community, which is specified in the treaty, though the basic list of crimes has been long recognized by the international community. And it is supposed to apply that law effectively and impartially to that political community. I will focus on the first and third dimensions of assessment and I will not comment on the second dimension of legitimacy, which has been the subject of interesting commentary to the extent that there is a worry that the ICC may engage in excessive lawmaking (Alvarez, 2005, chap. 9; Luban, 2011).

I keep the focus on the genuine possession of a moral power because the court whose legitimacy is in question here does not have a right to rule and it does not have coercive power. Coercive power is not really a live issue (Ladenson, 1990). The court issues directives that are meant to be binding primarily on state parties and that may be morally binding also on individuals in rebel armies. And it is this bindingness that is in question here. The court does not have a right to rule, persons or states do not owe compliance to the court. The court acts in the name of an international community and if there is anything to which a duty might be owed it would be to the international community as a whole that has established the court and the law. The International Criminal Court is essentially a subordinate institution in the context of the international community as courts are normally subordinate institutions.[1]

Arbitrary circumscription of jurisdiction

The problem is that the three most powerful military powers have not ratified the treaty establishing the court and so do not come under the legal jurisdiction of the court except if they commit crimes on the territory of a member state. But these powers seem to have committed crimes or at least there is plenty of warrant for an investigation. So, we can ask the question whether the failure to investigate, prosecute or try crimes by the major players in the international system implies a failure by the court to realize impartiality in the application of the most basic human rights norms to that system.

The quick response to this is to say that the ICC cannot fail to realize impartiality in areas where it has no legal jurisdiction. For example, we do not charge domestic courts with failures of justice when they do not try cases in other countries. Impartiality applies only within the legally specified jurisdiction. So why shouldn't we say the same thing about the ICC? If so, there is no failure of impartiality when persons who are members of states that are not parties to the treaty are not charged.

This is too quick. We must distinguish between the question of the legal basis of the limited jurisdiction and the question its political and moral justification. The legal legitimacy of an institution's actions is necessarily partly determined by its legal jurisdiction. It cannot be legally illegitimate for an institution to act solely within the confines of its legal jurisdiction. But this does not settle the case for the moral and political justification of an institution or whether the jurisdiction is wrongfully circumscribed. The principles of moral and political justification provide a standard outside the legal system by which to judge it.

Here are some analogous cases in which the legal jurisdiction of a court is arbitrarily circumscribed given the function of the court. Consider the failure of courts in the antebellum south of the US to try slaveholders for raping their slaves, in most cases for killing their slaves and more generally for failing to provide protection for slaves from their masters (Kolchin, 2003, p. 124). This failure accorded with the law but we think of it as a severe challenge to the moral justification of the court in addition to the law more generally. Think of the attitude of courts to marital rape and violence up through the nineteenth century. Again, this is, in significant part, a problem of the law of coverture, which gave men dominion over their wives. But in part, the idea was that the courts should not intervene in these kinds of cases 'to preserve the sanctity of the domestic circle' and in order to 'shut out the public gaze.'[2] These are only imperfect analogies but they do suggest something like the sense that some judicial or prosecutorial decisions involve an arbitrary circumscription of the jurisdiction of the court. Moreover, it is clear that international criminal law itself involves a massive expansion of the jurisdiction of international courts. The Nuremberg tribunal expanded the reach of courts to 'crimes against humanity,' committed by state actors in their own states. The criminal tribunals set up for Yugoslavia and Rwanda extended the jurisdiction to non-state actors (Teitel, 2011, chap 4). A restriction of the court's jurisdiction to state actors was thought to be indefensible. At the same time, we need not think that the jurisdictions of domestic courts are arbitrarily circumscribed, the reason being that other courts try crimes in other jurisdictions.

I assert that the jurisdiction of a criminal court is arbitrarily circumscribed when it does not have jurisdiction over a party if the following five conditions are met. First, the law the court applies is in pursuit of a morally mandatory aim of the political society. Second, the law it applies does apply to those parties or the law itself is arbitrarily circumscribed. Third, the party is an active participant both in the larger society of which the court is a part and in the activities of the court itself. Fourth, the party is an interested party with regard to the issues that are raised by the court. Fifth, no other court is willing and able to apply the law to that party.

These are meant to be jointly sufficient conditions, not necessary conditions. When these five conditions are met there is a fundamental inequality in the society: some are above the law (in the strong sense that they direct its application and benefit from impunity) while others are subject to it. The restriction of jurisdiction is a public expression of the unequal status of the different parties. Therefore, the jurisdiction of the court is arbitrarily circumscribed.

The ICC's jurisdiction is arbitrarily circumscribed in a way that diminishes its moral justification and ultimately damages its legitimacy because the basic conditions I enumerated above are met. I argue that the international community is a political community, partially unified around certain political institutions such as the United Nations and its various institutions such as the Security Council. These institutions create and apply law, and sometimes enforce it, in a way that implies that the law applies to all, in particular, international law prohibiting genocide, crimes against humanity, war crimes and the crime of aggression. Furthermore, much of this law is understood to be in pursuit of aims that all regard as morally mandatory such as international peace and security, protection of persons from widespread and profound human rights abuses, the avoidance of global environmental disaster, the alleviation of severe global poverty, among others.

That these are morally mandatory aims can be seen in two different ways. First, all or nearly all, states have committed themselves to the idea that they have duties to pursue these aims in various international agreements such as the Charter of the United Nations, the Millennium Declaration, the United Nations Framework Convention on Climate Change, and others. The great powers have all signed on to these documents. This is substantial evidence that these are mandatory aims of international society and it shows that they are recognized as such. Second, to the extent that we see the international system as a political system, pursuit of these aims is a minimum requirement for thinking that the system is concerned with the fundamental interests of all the persons that come under it. Thus, pursuit of these aims is a minimum condition of justification for the international political system.

First, the protection of persons from widespread human rights abuses has been recognized as a mandatory aim since the end of the Second World

War. It is enshrined in the Preamble and the first Article of the Charter of the United Nations. Furthermore, the crimes which the ICC is supposed to investigate are recognized by most as subjects of *jus cogens* norms, which are peremptory legal norms that apply to all states and that limit the legislative powers of states (Crawford, 2014, pp. 265, 369, 423; Weller, 2011, p. 189). They are asserted in many different legal documents from The Hague and Geneva Conventions, the Genocide Convention, the charters of various international criminal tribunals and international covenants on human rights.

Second, an essential part of the effort to protect persons from widespread human rights abuses is the establishment of criminal tribunals that are meant to call people to account and condemn these abuses. The United States is committed to the aim of protection of persons from serious violations of human rights. It is also committed to the need for an international criminal justice system for the investigation and prosecution of those violations as an essential means for pursuing this aim. The international community takes a general interest in the perpetration of the major crimes the ICC pursues and their punishment. This can be seen in the Security Council Resolution 1593 of 31 March 2005 referring the situation in Darfur to the Prosecutor of the ICC. Sudan is not a member of the ICC, but its actions are seen to come under the purview of the ICC. The Security Council's official reason concerning international peace and security suggests that situations in which there are large scale crimes against humanity, war crimes, genocide and aggression generally constitute threats to international peace and security.[3]

Thirdly, the United States is a major player in the international system both in relation to the international criminal court and in relation to the system as a whole. I will focus on the United States here on out since it satisfies these conditions most completely. The United States played a major role in shaping the ICC in the processes that led up to the signing of the Rome Statute, though it did not get everything it wanted. For example, it achieved some protection in Article 98 of the Rome Statute from arrest for its nationals when they carry out activities specified in Status of Forces Agreements in countries who have ratified the treaty. It got significant participation of the Security Council in the activities of the Court. And it does participate in the activities of the ICC inasmuch as it has allowed and, in one case, voted for the Security Council to refer cases to the ICC and cooperates with the ICC in a variety of ways (Bosco, 2014; Schabas, 2011, p. 34). And it is a major participant in the international community more generally.

Fourth, the United States is a deeply interested party in relation to the activities of the ICC. It engages in military and diplomatic activities in promotion of its interests as well as various moral and public goods around the world. Some of its activities either may involve commission of the crimes above or carry serious risks of committing some of the crimes described above.

Finally, the United States has not joined any other international criminal justice system that can enforce these elements of international criminal law against high ranking officials and it has shown no interest in even investigating high officials when there is evidence of criminal activity. Indeed, there may be the reason for it to avoid prosecution of high officials in the case of international crimes since this raises the stakes of politics too much (Walzer, 2010). For this reason, democratic societies may have strong reason to delegate this kind of activity to international courts.

Therefore, the current international system in which officials of the United States and the other great powers are not subject to the judgment of the International Criminal Court violates a fundamental moral and legal norm of equality among states and among persons in the international system.[4] The circumscription of jurisdiction is a kind of public embodiment of the treatment of some societies and persons as inferiors. Thus, an international criminal justice system that is inherently disabled from calling violators from certain states to account has its jurisdiction limited arbitrarily.

State consent and jurisdiction

Does the fact that some states have not consented to be subject to international criminal justice, even in the case of the most heinous crimes, defeat the thesis that the jurisdiction is arbitrarily circumscribed when it does not cover them? State consent is an important source of legitimacy because states are still the primary vehicles by which political power is accountable to persons in the international system and states are still the primary providers of the fundamental goods of justice, security and the public good to persons in the international system. States are the only major force that effectively makes the international community accountable to persons.

In addition, even if we recognize the morally mandatory character of the aims above, there is moral room for a state to refuse consent insofar as there is a great deal of uncertainty and reasonable disagreement about how to pursue the mandatory aims and even how to specify them. It is important for the international system to enable states to experiment with different ways of trying to specify and achieve those aims. States must be able to refuse certain forms of cooperation in order to pursue others. Hence, states will permissibly enter into diverse regional and sometimes even competing global agreements in order to pursue these mandatory aims. As long as states are making good faith efforts to pursue the mandatory aims in cooperation with others, they act permissibly even when they refuse consent to particular arrangements. Hence, the need for state consent is grounded in the importance of a sphere of liberty for states that can be justified by the morally mandatory aims.

But refusal of consent to treaties pursuing mandatory aims must be limited to good faith and reasonable disagreement about how to pursue the aims. This makes the system distinct from a system of merely voluntary association. A state's refusal of consent is unreasonable when it is based on mere unwillingness to shoulder the burdens as equals, irrationality, or a refusal to engage in compromise on issues on which people disagree and when it doesn't pursue alternative realistic options. These motives are inconsistent with a concern to pursue the morally mandatory aims in cooperation with others. So, state consent and the liberty to refuse consent have morally important and central roles to play in the international system but some forms of refusal are impermissible. It may be permissible to pressure unreasonable non-consenters into participation with the cooperative arrangement.

Jus cogens norms and the general principles of international law can invalidate particular acts of state consent. It does not seem a great stretch to suggest that there are moral limits on refusal of consent. We see this in domestic constitutional systems as well. Sometimes it is required for a government not only not to transgress constitutional norms but to make law that accords with constitutional norms.

So we have a political system because we have a group of states that are (1) duty-bound to cooperate in pursuit of morally mandatory aims, (2) there is reasonable disagreement about how to pursue these aims, which must be resolved by some kind of collective decision-making, (3) there are limits on what states may validly consent to and what grounds they may refuse consent on, (4) states are bound by their valid agreements. Hence, we have significant limitations on the sovereignty of states in this system (Christiano, 2017). I think this helps us make sense of the kind of pressure that is brought to bear by the international community on states that refuse to participate in nuclear non-proliferation arrangements. We see some basis here for the permission to impose trade sanctions on states that fail to cooperate in pursuing environmental aims (Barrett, 2005). We can also see why it makes sense to allow the Security Council to refer situations to the ICC even if the perpetrator and the territory are not of a state party to the Rome Statute. These reflect some commitment to the limits on state consent already implicit in the way the international system works. To be clear, I am not defending the particulars, only that they demonstrate the limits of the refusal of consent.

The ICC, and the international criminal justice system of which it is a part, since it is a key element in the effort to stop widespread human rights abuses, does depend for its legitimacy on the consent of states. But in the case of unreasonable refusal of consent and the absence of any alternative effort to pursue the same aim on the part of a state, the limit of the ICC's jurisdiction to states that have consented is morally arbitrary and this limit damages its moral and political legitimacy, or so I will argue.

Now it seems to me that there is something unreasonable in the refusal of the United States to ratify the Rome Statute. What the United States has consistently refused to do is allow international criminal tribunals to examine its own behavior. It refused to do this in the case of the International Criminal Tribunal for the former Yugoslavia even though the tribunal had jurisdiction over American activities. See, for instance, Carla Del Ponte's account that NATO forces could not be investigated by the prosecutor (Del Ponte, 2009, p. 60). It simply refuses to allow its high-level nationals to be investigated. The arguments it has given seem exceptionally weak. The arguments are of two forms. One argument is that the court's power is unchecked. What this means is unclear since there are a variety of checks on the powers of the Prosecutor and on the Court. The other is that this poses a challenge to the Security Council since it does not retain exclusive power to examine issues of widespread human rights abuses. But, the Security Council does retain a significant role in the operation of the ICC: it can refer cases and it can defer investigations. Both these arguments rely on the idea that there will be a chilling effect on the human rights protecting activities of the United States, since it could be prosecuted for serious crimes committed in pursuit of these activities (Goldsmith, 2006; Grossman, 2006). But this is an especially puzzling argument to make when the US constitutional system is built on the idea that the state must be constrained by justiciable law even when pursuing the protection of its population. Furthermore, there is no evidence of a good faith commitment to trying high officials for any of these serious international crimes. Finally, these points suggest an unreasonable unwillingness to compromise with other states on issues on which there is reasonable disagreement. The parties to the Rome Statute bent over backward to accommodate the concerns of the United States and it has refused to go along.

Because the ICC is currently constituted in a way that disables it from prosecuting and trying crimes of the world's great military powers, the ICC's jurisdiction is arbitrarily circumscribed. Here one takes the jurisdictional restrictions as an aspect of the ICC. The ICC is conceived of as a residual institution such that when other courts are unwilling or unable to try serious crimes, it has the role of trying these crimes. And it is clearly designed with an eye to having a kind of global jurisdiction.

I want to make two clarifications to this reasoning. I am not endorsing a principle of universal jurisdiction for the International Criminal Court (according to which the court has jurisdiction over all persons and territories regardless of whether a state has ratified the treaty), which principle was rejected by the parties to the Rome Statute. It is important that each state plays a role in shaping the court which has jurisdiction over it. This is a part of the grounds of the legitimacy of any court. In the case of unreasonable refusal to consent, states have a duty to join the court and may be pressured into joining the court. Perhaps in the event that they refuse to budge and they do not make alternative provisions for investigating and trying their nationals, a case can be made for extending jurisdiction over them. But this is a special case and does not imply a general principle of universal jurisdiction.

Furthermore, I do not think that there is an unqualified moral justification for an international court to act outside its legal jurisdiction. The political and legality conditions are still conditions of moral justification and ultimately legitimacy. I want to argue, however, that the system overall has a severe deficit of moral justification because of the arbitrary circumscription of jurisdiction. This leaves us with a kind of moral dilemma for the ICC or the international criminal justice system as a whole. On the one hand, the system suffers from a deficit of moral justification as a consequence of its invidiously circumscribed jurisdiction. On the other hand, no international criminal court in the system can be unqualifiedly justified in prosecuting the crimes of major powers since to do so would be to act outside its legal jurisdiction and hence violate the political condition of legitimacy. The logical consequence is that the court is damned if doesn't prosecute or investigate these crimes and it is damned if it does.

Equality and legitimacy

The most obvious threat to the justification of a moral power that some agent holds over others is that the arrangement does not treat the parties as equals. And the principle of political equality implies that all adult persons are to be treated politically as equals by the political and legal institutions of society. I will take the principle of equality as a fundamental moral principle and assume that holds sway in the contemporary international community. One basic problem of authority is: how can an institutionally defined agent that possesses the moral power to impose duties on others be compatible with treating persons politically as free and equal? The asymmetry of moral powers seems to suggest a fundamental inequality that is incompatible with the political equality of persons. We accept asymmetric powers (though within limits) in the parental relationship, in the relation of guardian to ward more generally and to some extent in the relation of society to proven criminals. But with ordinary adults, the asymmetry poses a problem (Locke, 1988, chap. 2).

This concern relates to legitimacy in particular when there is kind of radical inequality among the parties that leads persons unmistakably to see that they are treated as unequals. This is not mere injustice, though injustice it is. It is an injustice so blatant it that publicly expresses the inequality of the parties. When a political institution publicly embodies this inequality, the content independent reason giving character of its decisions is undercut for those who are treated as inferiors. They can no longer think that the source of the decision is one that includes them; it is simply the assertion of power of someone else over them.

An institutional agent that imposes duties on persons can be made minimally compatible with equality in three distinct ways, each of which is important for its legitimacy. First, it can treat people as equals in the processes by which it was established and by which the law it applies was created. In the case of courts in many domestic societies, they are established by the democratic process and they apply the law that has been made democratically.

Second, it can treat people as equals in the process by which authority is exercised. For example, is there an inherent bias in the structure of the institution or at least in the normal operation of the institution? An institution suffers a severe defect of legitimacy to the extent that some groups in society hold a great deal of power over the exercise of its authority while others are mostly just subject to it. This defect is all the greater when those who have greater power use it to protect themselves from its operation. This is a defect in the democratic credentials of the institution. And this defect damages the legitimacy of the institution even if the institution has been democratically created. Similarly, state consent is not sufficient to erase the stain of public inequality any more than individual consent erases the stain of exploitation.

Third, it can treat people as equals in the outcomes of the exercise of its authority. An institution can fail to exercise its authority in the content of its decisions as well as the process by which they come about. A democratic assembly, for example, can pass severely discriminatory laws against some group. In this way, it can fail to treat the members of the society as equals. A court can fail in a similar way. It can engage in the extremely selective application of law to the members of society in a way that seems to suggest the inferiority of one group relative to another.[5] In what follows, I will focus on the second and third concerns, which are essential parts of the idea of the rule of law.[6]

Two defects in the legitimacy of the ICC

Here I want to give two arguments for the defective legitimacy of the ICC by virtue of its arbitrarily circumscribed jurisdiction. First, the defective legitimacy of arbitrarily circumscribed jurisdiction has to do with the structure of the authority itself. The idea is that some are above the authority while others are subject to it. The major powers participate in the implementation of the law (through the Security Council and through their assistance to the ICC) and are interested in how that law is implemented and yet do not have the law applied to themselves. They participate in the process of imposing duties on others while they have little fear that any such duties are imposed on themselves.

These inequalities tie in with some traditional unjust inequalities that have a long and terrible history. Here the fact that all investigations (save one at the moment) have been of African persons should give us pause. It could be forgiven if someone thought that this was a kind of continuation of a long and disastrous colonial history. We are not merely speaking of someone being above the authority and others subject to it. We are speaking of powers that have traditionally been oppressive colonial or neocolonial powers being above the law and powers that have traditionally been colonized powers being subject to the law.

There are deep interests at stake in the activities of the court and these interests appear to be treated quite unequally by the court. For example, the court concerns itself with activities undertaken in civil wars or interstate wars and often in the context of ongoing conflict. Such criminal proceedings can change the dynamics of a conflict situation in a way that can interfere with the making of a political solution to the problem. Here the arbitrarily circumscribed jurisdiction of the ICC can take on special importance. It introduces an asymmetry into conflicts when some parties cannot be investigated and some can.

Suppose that the International Criminal Court has a deterrent effect on those who come under its jurisdiction as Hyeran Jo and Beth Simmons argue.[7] It can make a difference to the calculations of persons in deciding what to do. Now interstate and some intrastate conflicts are still sometimes solved by means of force. Sometimes force is used excessively by all the parties to the conflict to the extent that war crimes and crimes against humanity are committed. If the International Criminal Court can only investigate and try the parties on one side of the conflict, this works essentially to the advantage of the other party. It deters one party but not the other from acting to advance their interests. The interests of the disadvantaged party are set back relative to the advantaged party. I do not mean to say that any party has legitimate interests in perpetrating crimes against humanity or war crimes. It is nevertheless the case that they may be advancing legitimate interests in the conflict such as the protection of a certain minority from majority oppression, or a better distribution of resources among the various groups. The exercise of jurisdiction over one of the parties and the lack of jurisdiction over the other party is an important asymmetry of treatment that may alter the course of the conflict partly in favor of the party over which there is no jurisdiction. It may translate into military successes on the ground for the party that does not need to worry about being prosecuted. It may translate into increased bargaining power over the final negotiated settlement for one of the parties. These effects may translate into different capacities to achieve legitimate interests. When the asymmetry is systematically grounded in the fact that one of the parties is a major power and the other isn't, there is a relevant inequality that implies an inequality of concern for the interests of the different parties.

Another asymmetry is that the major powers may bring about laws or interpretations of law that are to be implemented by the ICC and which they would never accept to be applied to themselves but which are applied to others. Since they are exempt from prosecution, the burden is imposed on others but not themselves.

To conclude this argument, the circumscription of jurisdiction involves a clear set of advantages for some and thus is a public realization of inequality among persons. Even when no imbalance of advantages occurs, there is every appearance that they could so occur and thus it is publicly expressed that the status of those persons is above those of others. To the extent that the public expression of the equality of persons is one of the fundamental tests of legitimate authority in the modern world, this undermines the legitimacy of those directives (Christiano, 2012).

The second legitimacy worry is connected with the expressive or symbolic character of the investigation, trial and punishment. The ICC seems to be saying something like, crimes committed by those who are not members of the most powerful states are serious and it is condemning them, those committed by members of the major powers are not so serious and it does not condemn them. This is important for legitimacy because part of the basic point of the ICC is to condemn certain outrages against persons in the name of the whole of international society and to express solidarity with the victims. It expresses the international society's condemnation of the behavior in terms of the laws of that society (Duff, 2011; Scanlon, 2003). Of course, part of the purpose of a court is to punish offenders and thereby to deter them and others from committing the same crime. But it is also meant to communicate to all the gravity of the crime they have committed and reaffirm the dignity of the victims.[8]

The condemnatory effect of a verdict is significantly reduced when other similar crimes are not being prosecuted for no apparent reason other than that the criminals are nationals of the major powers. First, it suggests that the international community does not condemn the crime per se but only the commission of the crime by certain actors who are not members of major powers. And the international community is not expressing solidarity with the victims as such but only with those who are properly connected. The fundamental message the international community is concerned with sending is that grave crimes against human beings are to be condemned and the victims in some way vindicated. But this cannot be so clear in the case of such a systematically biased court. Second, it suggests that it is not the international community per se that condemns the action. For the international community's action must take on an impartial character. It cannot single out some violations of a law as condemnable merely on the basis of who these persons are. For condemnation to be in the name of the international community it must be one that attends a crime because it is a violation of the law of that international community. But this is partly defeated when only some violators of the law are condemned, ones who are not powerful and where the explanation of this selection is rooted in the very structure of the court.

The consequences of these two observations are that the expression of condemnation and solidarity is muted or uncertain. Since the punishment is in part justified because it is such an expression, the justification is lessened and the reasons given to parties are weakened. Furthermore, when the condemnation is not clearly impartial, instead of acting in the name of a community of equals, the court seems to be operating more as the agent of a particular group that is imposing its will on others. Those who are not in that particular group are asked to be participants in the activity of condemnation, as if the condemnation proceeded from them. This is especially hard in the case where they disagree with the court's decisions. But it can be made legitimate if they genuinely participate as equals in the process by which condemnation is achieved and the process is impartial. When it isn't, those who disagree have reason to wonder why they should go along.

Objections

One objection to my thesis is that the perpetrators of the heinous crimes do not have anything to complain about when they have been prosecuted (Altman & Wellman, 2009, pp. 92–93). They have committed terrible crimes and so they are liable to punishment and cannot complain that the prosecution is not even-handed. There is something right about this objection, but it is not quite right. As I noted above the prosecution often inserts itself into intense conflict zones in which often all the different parties have been mistreated and at the same time have legitimate interests in bringing the conflict to a negotiated solution. When one of the parties is prosecuted the legitimate interests of those persons who are represented by the faction can be set back by this action and even the legitimate interests of the perpetrators can be set back. They have a complaint if they are not treated impartially because their interests are not being given equal consideration. The other party is free to act with impunity while they are not.

One might object that my reasoning only shows that the United States is acting in an illegitimate way and that the ICC cannot be faulted for this. Hence the ICC's legitimacy is not at stake here. I disagree; we must think of international institutions as deriving their identities in part from the states that make them work. The United States is a major player in how the ICC works. It played a major role in shaping it; it plays a major role in the intelligence gathering; it plays a major role in shaping who the prosecutor investigates and it plays a major role in the Security Council process of referral of cases to the ICC (Bosco, 2014; Thakur, 2014; Tiemessen, 2014). It must be seen as part of the system of the ICC. Hence the legitimacy of the United States and the ICC are bound together in this instance.

A related objection is that I am asking the ICC to do something that it cannot do. How can one impugn the legitimacy of an institution on the basis of facts it cannot do anything about? In general, I do not think feasibility in the special sense meant here is essential to the properties that make an institution legitimate. We do not say that a non-democratic regime is legitimate after all because the elites running it refuse to give up power as they ought, thus making it unfeasible for us to realize its legitimacy on our own. The problem of the ICC is simply that some of the major players in its operation refuse to do their duty and submit to it as others do. It is perfectly feasible for the United States to do what it must do and join as a full-fledged member, it just does not do it. But since it is so much a part of the ICC's operation, this impugns the ICC itself.[9]

Possible qualifications

These arguments need not imply that the court's actions give no reasons for compliance; it may still stand up to some extent for the long-term hope of realizing the rule of law and criminal justice.[10] It may still correctly convict and condemn persons who ought to be convicted and condemned. It may still be capable of some deterrence and thus may protect some people from terrible treatment. It may represent some progress over the past (Goldston, 2010). Of course, all of these considerations need to be empirically assessed and we do not have a great deal of information about the effectiveness of the court even in the situations in which it is allowed to operate.

So, there may be some reasons to go along with the verdicts of the court despite the weaknesses I have described, but those reasons are weak ones in the sense that they can be relatively easily overridden in the case of disagreement with the verdicts of the court.

Conclusion

I have argued that the circumscription of the jurisdiction of the International Criminal Court is arbitrary and that this diminishes the legitimacy of the court. It may not extinguish the legitimacy of the Court because it does perform important tasks. But it is important to gauge the damage to legitimacy that can arise from invidiously determined limits to jurisdiction. This may help explain the increasing unwillingness of many African states and of the African Union to cooperate with the ICC, despite the fact that they were once among its strongest supporters. My guess is that the best way to enhance the legitimacy of the ICC would be, in addition to ceasing its invidiously selective approach to prosecution, for the United States to join it as a full member. This is certainly eminently feasible for the US and it would enhance both its own legitimacy as well as that of the ICC.

Notes

1. For these three kinds of legitimacy, see Christiano (2008, chap. 6).
2. See Opinion in STATE v. RICHARD OLIVER SUPREME COURT OF NORTH CAROLINA, RALEIGH 70 N.C. 60 January 1874.
3. See Resolutions and Decisions of the Security Council 1 August 2004–31 July 2005 (New York: United Nations, 2005) pp. 131–132 for the key document.
4. See Crawford (2014) pp. 368–69 for the evidence that the principle of equality of persons before the law and to the protection of the law is a fundamental principle of international law.
5. See Christiano (2008) chapters 6 and 7 for the development. I set aside here instrumentalist conceptions of authority. The comparative benefit account does not give an account of how content-independent reasons can arise from the comparative benefit of the institution. I criticize the NJT in Christiano (2008, pp. 233–34). Both of these accounts provide, at best, weak reasons for complying when one disagrees strongly with a decision, hence they do not serve well the disagreement mediating function of legitimate authority.
6. See Pavel (this issue) for further discussion of the rule of law and legitimacy.
7. See for a defense of the deterrent effects of the ICC see Jo and Simmons (2016) and Sikkink (2011). For some skepticism see Mark Drumbl (2007) and Deidre Golash (Golash, 2010).
8. For more on the relation between the purpose of an institution and its legitimacy see Scherz and Zysset, Schmelzle, and Adams (all this issue).
9. For more on feasibility and international institutions see Erman and Kuyper (this issue).
10. Judith Shklar (1964) argues that while the Nuremberg Trials violated the rule of law, they also promoted it.

Acknowledgments

I would like to thank Nathan Adams, Samantha Besson, Antoinette Scherz, Cord Schmelzle, Andrew Williams, Alain Zysset and the referees for CRISSP for helpful comments and discussion of previous drafts of this paper.

Disclosure statement

No potential conflict of interest was reported by the author.

References

Altman, A., & Wellman, C. (2009). *A liberal theory of international justice.* Oxford: Oxford University Press.
Alvarez, J. (2005). *International organizations as law makers.* Oxford: Oxford University Press.
Barrett, S. (2005). *Environment and statecraft.* Cambridge: Cambridge University Press.
Bosco, D. (2014). *Rough justice: The international criminal court in a world of power politics.* Oxford: Oxford University Press.
Christiano, T. (2008). *The constitution of equality: Democratic authority and its limits.* Oxford: Oxford University Press.
Christiano, T. (2012). The legitimacy of international institutions. In A. Marmor (Ed.), *Routledge companion to the philosophy of law* (pp. 380–394). London: Routledge.
Christiano, T. 2017. 'Democracy, migration and international institutions' In J. Knight (Ed.), *NOMOS LVII: Immigration, emigration and migration* (pp. 239–276).
Crawford, J. (2014). *Chance, order, change: The course of international law.* The Hague: Hague Academy of International Law.
Del Ponte, C. (2009). *Madame prosecutor: Confrontations with humanity's worst criminals and the culture of impunity.* New York: Other Press.
Drumbl, M. (2007). *Atrocity, punishment and international law.* Cambridge: Cambridge University Press.
Duff, A. (2011). Authority and responsibility in international criminal law. In S. Besson & J. Tasioulas (Eds.), *The philosophy of international law* (pp. 589–604). Oxford: Oxford University Press.
Golash, D. (2010). The justification of punishment in the international context. In L. May & Z. Hoskins (Eds.), *International criminal law and philosophy* (pp. 201–223). Cambridge: Cambridge University Press.
Goldsmith, J. (2006). The self-defeating international criminal court. In R. Lillich, H. Hannum, S. J. Anaya, & D. L. Shelton (Eds.), *International human rights: Problems of law, policy, and practice* (4th ed., pp. 931–936) University of Chicago Law Review 70 (2003) New York: Aspen.
Goldston, J. (2010). More candour about criteria: The exercise of discretion by the international criminal court. *Journal of International Criminal Justice, 8,* 383–406.
Grossman, M., (Under-Secretary of State for Political Affairs, US Department of State). (2006). American foreign policy and the international criminal court,' remarks to the center for strategic and international studies. In May 6, 2002 (Eds.), R. Lillich, H. Hannum, S. J. Anaya, & D. L. Shelton. *International human rights: Problems of law, policy, and practice* (4th ed., pp. 928–931) Washington D.C, New York: Aspen.
Jo, H., & Simmons, B. (2016). Can the international criminal court deter atrocity? *International Organization.*
Kolchin, P. (2003). *American slavery 1619–1877.* New York: Hill and Wang.

Ladenson, R. (1990). In defense of a hobbesian conception of law. In J. Raz (Ed.), *Authority* (pp. 32–55). New York: NYU Press.

Locke, J. (1988). The second treatise on civil government. In P. Laslett (Ed.), *Two treatises on civil government* (3rd ed., pp. 265–428). Cambridge: Cambridge University Press.

Luban, D. (2011). Fairness to rightness: Jurisdiction, legality and the legitimacy of international criminal law. In S. Besson & J. Tasiolas (Eds.), *The philosophy of international law* (pp. 569–588). Oxford: Oxford University Press.

Raz, J. (1986). *The morality of freedom*. Oxford: Oxford University Press. Rome Statute.

Scanlon, T. M. (2003). Punishment and the rule of law. In T. M. Scanlon (Ed.), *The difficulty of tolerance: Essays in political philosophy* (pp. 219–233). Cambridge: Cambridge University Press.

Schabas, W. A. (2011). *An introduction to the international criminal court* (4th ed.). Cambridge: Cambridge University Press.

Shklar, J. (1964). *Legalism: Law, morals and political trials*. Cambridge: Harvard University Press.

Sikkink, K. (2011). *The justice cascade: How human rights prosecutions are changing world politics*. New York: W.W. Norton & Company.

Simmons, A. J. (2000). Justification and legitimacy. In A. J. Simmons (Ed.), *Justification and legitimacy: Essays on rights and obligations* (pp. 122–157). Cambridge: Cambridge University Press.

Teitel, R. (2011). *Humanity's law*. Oxford: Oxford University Press.

Thakur, R. (2014). International criminal justice: At the vortex of power, norms and a shifting world order. In C. Sampford & R. Thakur (Eds.), *Institutional supports for the international rule of law* (pp. 30–58). Taylor and Francis: London.

Tiemessen, A. (2014). The international criminal court and the politics of prosecutions. *The International Journal of Human Rights, 18*(4–5), 444–461.

Walzer, M. 2010. 'Trying political leaders,' *New Republic* May 20th.

Weller, M. (2011). The struggle for an international constitutional order. In D. Armstrong (Ed.), *Routledge handbook of international law* (pp. 179–194). Abingdon: Routledge.

The UN Security Council, normative legitimacy and the challenge of specificity

Antoinette Scherz and Alain Zysset

ABSTRACT
This paper discusses how the general and abstract concept of legitimacy applies to international institutions, using the United Nations Security Council as an example. We argue that the evaluation of the Security Council's legitimacy requires considering three significant and interrelated aspects: its purpose, competences, and procedural standards. We consider two possible interpretations of the Security Council's purpose: on the one hand, maintaining peace and security, and, on the other, ensuring broader respect for human rights. Both of these purposes are minimally morally acceptable for legitimacy. Second, we distinguish between three different competences of the UNSC: 1) the decision-making competence, 2) the quasi-legislative competence, and 3) the referral competence. On this basis, we argue that different procedural standards are required to legitimise these competences, which leads to a more differentiated understanding of the Security Council's legitimacy. While maintaining that the membership structure of the Council is a severe problem for its legitimacy, we suggest other procedural standards that can help to improve its overall legitimacy, which include broad transparency, deliberation, and the revisability of the very terms of accountability themselves.

Introduction

The United Nations Security Council's (UNSC) legitimacy has been severely criticised for a variety of reasons. The most prominent critiques are centred on the anachronistic composition of its membership structure and its inefficiency in sustaining international peace and security in the face of long-lasting and deadly conflicts, such as most recently in Syria. But what does it mean to question the legitimacy of an international institution, and when are these legitimacy critiques justified? Legitimacy can be understood as an empirical or a normative concept. There have been different studies examining the sociological legitimacy of the UNSC, as a legitimacy belief or as authority influencing states' behaviour (e.g. Binder & Heupel, 2015; Cronin & Hurd, 2008; Hurd, 1999; Voeten, 2005). The literature on the normative legitimacy of international institutions is booming. Since Dahl's (1999) critical contribution, political theorists have developed and refined the standards that confer legitimacy on international institutions (e.g. Buchanan, 2013; Buchanan & Keohane, 2006; Grant & Keohane, 2005; Macdonald, 2016). In this literature, the concept of legitimacy is often understood as the 'right to rule' (cf. Raz, 1986). Recent contributions have sought to render the traditionally state-centred understanding of this concept applicable to international institutions (e.g. Besson, 2014; Buchanan & Keohane, 2006; Tasioulas, 2010). However, most accounts of legitimacy remain highly abstract, which makes their application to a specific international institution difficult.

This paper seeks to further clarify the concept of international legitimacy and show how it can be applied to the UNSC specifically. To this end, we draw on the 'meta-coordination view' of legitimacy (Buchanan, 2013, pp. 174–195; 2018). The paper offers an illustration of this account of international legitimacy and contributes to a more applied understanding of legitimacy theory. In the first part, we outline our account of the legitimacy of international institutions. We argue that international institutions have to fulfil different standards depending on their purpose and competences in order to provide sufficient, content-independent reasons to comply and not to interfere in order to be legitimate. Therefore, we examine three significant and interrelated aspects of the UNSC: first, the purpose of the UNSC; second, its institutional competences; and third, its procedural standards.

In the second part, we reconstruct two diverging but minimally acceptable readings of the purpose of the UNSC in the relevant literature in international relations and international law, namely international peace and security on the one hand, and the protection of human rights on the other. For this analysis, we concentrate on the question of whether the purpose of the UNSC fulfils minimal moral standards and leave aside the questions of its effectiveness and comparative benefits vis-à-vis other feasible institutions. In the third part of the paper, we distinguish three different competences of the UNSC: 1) *decision-making* competence; 2) *quasi-legislative* competence; and 3) *referral* competence. Finally, in the fourth part, we argue for reforms of the procedural legitimacy standards of the UNSC on the basis of its purpose and competences. We start by discussing membership amendments on the basis of delegation and participation models of accountability. For reasons of feasibility, we shift the focus to other procedural standards for the outlined competences and argue that the procedural standards for the newer ones are particularly lacking.

The concept and standards of legitimacy for international institutions

The concept of legitimacy as the 'right to rule' is considered to provide sufficient, content-independent reason for compliance.[1] The meta-coordination view is based on the understanding that coercion is not sufficient to make institutions efficient, but that voluntary compliance is required, at least to some degree. Buchanan argues that before coordination through an institution is possible, it is necessary to converge on *how to decide* which of the different possible institutional alternatives we should coordinate our behaviour around (Buchanan, 2013, pp. 174–195, 2018). The meta-coordination view understands legitimacy as addressing this problem by providing standards that are reason-based, falling into the space between self-interest and justice. Legitimacy forms part of non-ideal theory as it provides institutional standards under circumstances of profound disagreement about justice but where coordination through institutions is necessary to move towards justice (Buchanan & Keohane, 2006, p. 412). The meta-coordination view places most of its weight on assessable procedural standards and is therefore epistemically more accessible than a Razian account (Raz, 1986) that relies on objective reasons over which disagreement might arise.

Justifying political power with regard to equal autonomy

On the meta-coordination view, legitimacy provides a risk-benefit analysis that includes moral considerations (Buchanan, 2013, p. 190). Yet what constitutes the relevant risks and benefits remains mostly undefined. In our opinion, institutions that exercise authority through rules that demand compliance generate special risks and benefits for the autonomy of their subjects. The conception of legitimacy that we propose is a specification of the meta-coordination view based on the fundamental notion of equal autonomy, including both individual and collective autonomy (e.g. Habermas, 1996, Chapter 3; Forst, 2012, pp. 125–137). However, other readings – for example, those based on non-domination or equal consideration of interests – might also be used. We focus on political institutions because they do not just narrow the option set of others, but also affect their status as norm-givers. Therefore, the claim to political power, i.e. authority, through rules is specifically normatively problematic. However, it is different from brute force insofar as it addresses those subjected to the rules and demands their compliance. In this sense, authorities enter into a form of discourse in which they strive to justify why their rules should count as sufficient, content-independent reasons for action to autonomous subjects. On this basis, we define legitimacy as the requirement to provide sufficient, content-independent reasons to comply and not to interfere with an institution's rules, compatible with equal autonomy.

As a value of political institutions, legitimacy applies to institutions with rule-setting authority, including rule application and possibly some form of enforcement. In a system of rules, it is not only the enforcing agency that exercises political power, but the combination of the legislative, executive, and judiciary that creates the systematic capacity to restrict autonomy. Therefore, legitimacy judgements evaluate the justification of political power through both the setting and the application of rules, which refers to taking decisions that are supported by and embedded within a system of rules or a treaty. We understand rules as applicable to a class of individuals or organisations as general standards of behaviour. The international system is, however, highly fragmented, which means that these functions can be more dispersed, though they can also exhibit less of a separation of powers than within the state. The Security Council is such an institution because it operates within the framework of the UN Charter and issues resolutions that can claim to be binding on all UN Members.

Our concept of legitimacy also comprises a non-ideal dimension. Non-ideal theory is especially relevant at the international level because it takes into account feasibility restrictions. Currently, we are faced with an international system structured in different states that are not all democratic. Assuming that, for normative and pragmatic reasons, it is not possible to force states either to become democracies or to establish a democratic, state-like federation without their consent, a fully democratic international system is not achievable in the short- or medium-term. Therefore, such an ideal alone cannot guide which institutions we should comply with. As such, legitimacy for international institutions needs to include non-ideal standards that consider how to move from current conditions towards an ideal. In a multilevel framework, international institutions cannot and should not be thought to compensate for a lack of democracy on the domestic level. However, taking the conditions of individual and collective autonomy as the basis for legitimacy establishes two minimal requirements for international institutions. First, taking human rights norms as a baseline for individual autonomy, an institution continuously or even systematically violating these norms cannot be legitimate. Second, international institutions should neither threaten democracy in already democratic states, nor prevent democratic development in non-democratic ones.

Graded standards of legitimacy

International institutions vary vastly in their purposes, the range of authority they claim in carrying out these purposes, and the effects they generate. Given such variety, which legitimacy standards are appropriate for international institutions? We argue that international institutions have to fulfil different standards of legitimacy depending on their specific purpose(s) and competences in rule-setting and application. Based on these parameters, legitimacy standards help international institutions to generate sufficient reasons for compliance with their rules by minimising the threat to the autonomy of those subjected to them.

First, the purpose of an institution is itself part of what makes it legitimate. Certain institutional purposes are not compatible with securing the conditions of equal autonomy regardless of their effects. For example, the purpose of a murder guild violates autonomy even if the guild does not actually kill anyone. Therefore, minimal moral acceptability should be regarded as a necessary requirement for legitimacy (cf. Buchanan & Keohane, 2006, Adams this issue).[2] Beyond this restriction, different purposes can be more or less important for the protection of autonomy and accordingly generate more or less weighty reasons for compliance. Furthermore, institutions should be judged on the basis of how effective they are in achieving their purpose. On the one hand, this is necessary for institutions to generate a benefit compared to non-institutional alternatives, in order to mitigate the risk of empowering an institution in the first place. This is often captured in terms of effectiveness. On the other hand, whether institutions also have to create benefits compared to other feasible institutional alternatives is debatable (e.g. Buchanan, 2013, p. 178). In our opinion, they need to create at least some additional benefits when compared with other *clearly* feasible institutions so as to be legitimate. Otherwise, legitimacy cannot achieve its meta-coordinative function. However, feasibility also restricts what can be demanded from an institution to be legitimate. Finally, an institution's purpose(s) and competences are closely connected since the competences needed for an institution heavily depend on its purpose. An institution's purpose also influences the kind of standards they should fulfil because the different functions (e.g. legislative, judicative or executive) aim at different benefits and create specific risks, which can be supported or constrained by different procedures.

Second, the kind and degree of competences influences the legitimacy standards required for international institutions. The risk to both individual and collective autonomy created by international institutions ultimately depends on the political power of the particular institution in question. Therefore, graded legitimacy standards should be applied. This means that the more political power, i.e. rule-setting and application competences, an international institution wields, the more demanding procedural legitimacy standards this institution has to meet. Different dimensions of political power determine an institution's capacity to affect the autonomy of its subjects. In particular, these dimensions include the scope of its rules, its domain sensitivity, and its rule applicability.[3] The legitimacy burden for institutions increases if any of these dimensions is extended. The first two dimensions concern the width and depth of the institution's rule-setting and application domain. The accumulation of rules – even concerning relatively technical issues – can restrict autonomy. Third, the domain sensitivity or depth considers the issues that can be affected by the institution and how important these are for autonomy. The applicability of rules can be direct or indirect. Since directly applicable rules do not require the agreement of states for their implementation, they remove the protection level of domestic institutions for individuals and collective autonomy.

While Buchanan and Keohane (2006) propose minimal standards for the legitimacy of international institutions, our approach seeks to determine specific standards for specific institutions depending on their competences. As Bodansky puts it, 'the basis of legitimacy of the Security Council may similarly vary depending on whether it is making a decision in an individual case or acting in a quasi-legislative capacity by promulgating more general rules' (2008, p. 316). The higher the competences, the stronger the procedural standards required to protect against the risks of undermining the autonomy of all UN Member States and citizens in their capacity for self-determination. The traditional way of thinking about how to make competence delegation compatible with autonomy is through accountability standards. Transparency should be regarded as a general legitimacy standard since it is a precondition for accountability. Furthermore, attaching standards to the creation or pedigree of an institution is another way to secure accountability. As far as international institutions are concerned, state consent is the main standard used in trying to achieve this. In this paper, however, we will not discuss the normative advantages and issues related to this standard. Instead, we will focus on the revisability of the terms of accountability, which is particularly pertinent if an institution's competences change.

Third, the overall legitimacy of an institution results from a sufficient balance of reasons between the risks and benefits for autonomy. On the one hand, the risk is created by the institution's political power, i.e. its competences and the process of its creation. On the other, three factors contribute to the positive reasons for compliance: first, the importance of its purpose for autonomy; second, its comparative benefits in achieving said purpose; third, the justification of its competences through procedural legitimacy standards.

In other words, an institution with a very important purpose but only weak procedural standards might still provide sufficient reasons to be legitimate. For example, Christiano argues that institutions that fulfil morally mandatory aims do not require state consent (2012 and in this issue). Vice versa, procedural standards may provide reasons to comply with institutions that do not function wholly efficiently or efficaciously. The overall sufficiency of reasons to comply constitutes legitimacy as a *threshold*. However, the feasibility of institutional alternatives relevant for both efficiency and procedural standards can shift this threshold considerably (to the point where the non-institutional option would prevail). Since epistemic uncertainties, particularly regarding feasibility, need to be taken into account, it is still important to consider which procedural standards help to shift the balance in favour of legitimacy.

In the next section, we evaluate the purpose of the UNSC by discussing its importance for autonomy and minimal moral acceptability. Discussing its effectiveness and comparative benefits would require an in-depth empirical analysis of the UNSC's performance, which goes beyond the scope of the present paper. That said, it is clear that the UNSC faces some notable challenges in this respect. One of the largest problems of the UNSC's effectiveness is not its action, but its inaction (cf. Berdal, 2003, p. 26; Buchanan & Keohane, 2011, pp. 48, 51). The ability to control the unauthorised use of force – in particular by the US – remains another central issue (cf. Malone, 2004; Weiss, 2003).[4] Finally, since the UNSC forms part of a bigger organisation, the checks and balances in the UN system, in particular its relationship to the General Assembly (GA), are also relevant for its legitimacy but go beyond the scope of this paper. Due to these restrictions, we cannot provide an all-things-considered assessment of the UNSC's legitimacy. Rather, we focus on the UNSC's competences in order to determine procedural standards of legitimacy that can contribute to improving the balance of reasons.

Two readings of the UNSC's purpose: beyond the letter of the UN charter

How should the purpose of an institution be defined? Formally, the purpose of the UNSC is defined by the UN Charter. Since our aim here is not to produce an in-depth analysis of the effectiveness of the UNSC, but rather to provide a normative evaluation of its purpose, we start with the explicit purpose as stated in Article 24 of the UN Charter, namely the Council's 'primary responsibility for the maintenance of international peace and stability'. This purpose sets it apart from the League of Nations' unspecified mandate. This purpose has to be interpreted in light of its evolutive practice. While initially aiming at resolving inter-state conflicts, the UNSC has resorted to Chapter VII of the UN Charter to address intra-state conflicts or non-military issues, whether national, regional or global. The scope of the UNSC's mandate in this domain is 'broad, if not virtually unfettered or unlimited, other than by the purpose and principles of the Charter, themselves broadly defined' (Shraga, 2011, p. 12).

Discussing how one should understand the UNSC's purpose of 'maintaining and restoring international peace and stability' in more detail is therefore necessary to assess its importance and the requirement of minimal moral acceptability. We suggest that the UNSC's evolving practice pursues two broad goals: (1) the 'classical' maintenance of peace and stability, and (2) the protection of human rights. Clearly, these two purposes are not mutually exclusive.

One reading confines the purpose to the UNSC's founding but evolutive aim of the maintenance of international peace and security. Two classical types of resolutions grounded in Chapter VI more concretely illustrate this first reading: peace-keeping and peace-building operations. The former, for instance, comprises the military observation of ceasefires following inter-state wars, while the latter, for instance, includes the reintegration of former soldiers into society or the rebuilding of rule of law institutions (legislative, judiciary, executive). Clearly, securing the interest(s) of states in security, peace, sovereignty, and self-determination remains the core normative value behind this reading. Interestingly, David Bosco suggests dividing this initial broad reading into two more specific sub-readings: the *concert* one, and the *governance* model. The *governance* model suggests that, moving from the original and formal mandate of preventing and managing inter-state conflict, the UNSC's purpose is to effectively address the external and novel threats to international peace and security, such as epidemic diseases or climate change. The 'securitisation' of the HIV/AIDS epidemic on the UNSC's agenda – such as the most recent 2011 resolution on the role of peace-keepers as vectors of HIV (Res. 1983 (2011)) – would be an illustrative example. Bosco does not, however, circumscribe the domain of 'governance' itself in clear terms (2014, p. 546). In contrast, the *concert* variant exclusively focuses on facilitating diplomatic negotiation between the five permanent members of the UNSC (United States, United Kingdom, France, Russia, and China) and therefore restricts the interest(s) at stake to this restricted circle: 'a concert perspective shifts the focus from the body's ability to resolve external challenges to its impact on relations between permanent members' (Bosco, 2014, p. 546). This *concert* view is reinforced by a consensualist decision-making process rather than a majority or super-majority: 'among the permanent members, the veto ensures that the Council is consensus-based' (Bosco, 2014, pp. 548–549).

At the other end of the spectrum, a far more challenging reading of the UNSC's purpose extends the purpose to the protection of human rights – a view that has been more developed by legal scholars. We suggest viewing this aim as *individuals-oriented* as it is individuals, but not necessarily states, that benefit from this much wider purpose. Although the UNSC is not a party to the main human rights treaties (such as the ICCPR), the unavoided atrocities of the post-Cold War era (former Yugoslavia, Rwanda, East Timor, and Sierra Leone), the subsequent formalisation of the Responsibility to Protect doctrine (Res. 1674 (2006)) and the expansion of UN-mandated bodies (ECOSOC, Human Rights Council, UN treaty bodies) have carved out a novel role for the UNSC to address intra-state or internal conflicts and use the language of human rights to articulate policies. Scholars of the UNSC speak of a 'normative shift' (Hassler, 2012 p. 28) or 'paradigm shift' (Rodley, 2015, p. 776) despite the fierce debate on the legality of humanitarian intervention. Legally, one can argue that human rights – through their growing recognition and implementation by Member

States – have become general principles of international law (in the meaning of Article 38(1) of the ICJ Statute) applicable to international organisations that exercise 'governmental authority' (Sarooshi, 1999, p. 16). Endorsing the states' implementation efforts would then fuel the very definition of international peace and security. As Shraga puts it, 'a conceptual link was thus established between human rights and international peace and security, or between their serious, systematic and massive violations and the existence of a threat to the peace' (2011, p. 12).

It soon becomes apparent that these two readings fulfil the requirement of minimal moral acceptability set out above. Both aim at securing a basic form of personal and collective autonomy through the protection from state-sponsored atrocities against individuals (personal autonomy) and/or by ensuring the state's capacity to exercise external sovereignty through non-interference (collective autonomy). In fact, these purposes are more than merely acceptable; they are of fundamental importance in creating and preserving the conditions for autonomy. However, one may interpret the purpose of an institution too charitably if one only takes into account official statements and regulations. Those in power might use institutions to further their interests while framing the purpose of the institution as a public good. It is important to keep this issue in mind while discussing how the institution's purpose is actually implemented. A further caveat is in order here: the minimal condition for *equal* autonomy in fulfilling its purpose means that an institution should at least not create new, or sustain severe existing, inequalities. Whether the UNSC fulfils this condition remains highly questionable.[5]

The changing competences of the UNSC

The political power of an institution understood as *rule-setting and applying competences* have to be justified to those subjected to its rules in order to be legitimate. Since higher competences pose a higher risk to autonomy, stronger procedural safeguards are required. We understand 'competences' as the legal mandate that is conferred on the institution by means of treaty law and its interpretation in practice. This concept captures the principled authority that the institution claims and the *de facto* use of authority that may overstep these claims. It appears that the terms of the treaty have been filled by the situations to which it has been applied, which are documented in the resolutions that the UNSC is empowered to generate.

On this basis, we distinguish three different competences of the UNSC. First, the UNSC has the narrow and exclusive competence to determine the creation, deployment, and use of military force in international relations in a system structured by the default principle of non-intervention in domestic affairs (UN Charter Article 2(4)). The procedural conditions for resorting to military force are enshrined in Chapter VII of the UN Charter. It must be borne in mind, however, that Chapter VI offers various non-military measures that should be primarily exhausted (peace settlement measures). The collective security system serves an interest that all Member States share, namely the protection of their autonomy vis-à-vis external interferences – an interest that the UN Charter refers to as 'the territorial integrity or political independence of any state' (Article 2(4)). Now, Member States can resort to military force without the UNSC's authorisation, but only within the scope fixed by the same charter, namely self-defence (Article 51). Once the UNSC is seized, however, the right to self-defence is suspended. The political power that the Security Council exercises by adopting resolutions with a primarily executive character is what we call the *decision-making* competence of the UNSC. The Charter also establishes corresponding responsibilities on the part of its subjects (all UN Member States) in Article 25: 'the Members of the United Nations agree to accept and carry out the decisions of the UNSC in accordance with the present Charter'. This means that the decisions and resolutions of the UNSC enjoy the status of binding obligations upon all UN Member States as a matter of international law. Within this competence, the UNSC can resort to a variety of softer tools to undertake its mandate. Chapter VI of the Charter encourages and recommends peaceful settlements of disputes (Articles 33–38), while Chapter VII of the Charter allows for a range of sanctions: forcible sanctions (Article 40) or economic and other non-forcible sanctions (Article 41). In accordance with Article 28 of the Charter, the UNSC can create a variety of subsidiary bodies as needed for the performance of its functions. These include committees, working groups, investigative bodies, international tribunals, peacekeeping operations, political missions, and the Peacebuilding Commission as an advisory, subsidiary organ.

Second, its competences apply to a broad and indeterminate domain, namely all threats to international peace and security – a domain that the UNSC has the exclusive (and legally recognised) latitude to define. As Bosco puts it, 'the Charter makes no geographic or qualitative distinction between potential disruptions to the peace and makes clear that the Council can investigate any dispute it deems dangerous to peace and security' (2014, p. 546). This indeterminacy leads to what we refer to as the *quasi-legislative* competence conferred to the UNSC by the UN Charter itself. This means that the UNSC can create law through resolutions that include general and abstract norms incurring binding obligations on states (cf. Tsagourias, 2011). There is ongoing debate about how far this quasi-legislative competence goes and whether it reaches beyond the issues of terrorism and weapons of mass destruction (e.g. Res. 1373 (2001) and 1540 (2004); (cf. Neusüss, 2008; Hassler, 2012, p. 16). However, these two cases show that the UNSC has the capacity to act through competences that are broad and that resemble those of a legislative body.

Third, according to Article 13(b) of the Rome Statute in conjunction with Chapter VII of the UN Charter, the UNSC can refer situations to the International Criminal Court (ICC). This third capacity is what we call the *referral competence* of the UNSC. In general, ICC investigations can only take place in UN Member States that are state parties to the Rome Treaty (2002). However, the referral enables prosecutions in situations outside the Court's treaty-based territorial and national jurisdiction. While we cannot address this referral competence and practice in detail here, suffice it to say that it signals the growing role of the UNSC in addressing basic interests of individuals at the expense of state authority. Indeed, international crimes concern the large-scale and systematic crimes committed by individuals belonging to or in position of public authority (Zysset, 2016).

In conclusion, the UNSC has developed its rule-setting and applying competences far beyond a narrow understanding of collective security limited to non-interference and international peace. Even though its resolutions have no *direct effect* in the legal sense – meaning that its decisions are not immediately valid in the domestic legal order – and although the UNSC's decisions leave a wide degree of discretion to states to determine the appropriate course of action, its potential capacity to restrict state autonomy is severe. The UNSC issues resolutions that are directly binding on UN members, and even though its competences may not concern a very wide set of issues, the issues in question lie at the heart of autonomy considerations. First, security or the protection of basic human rights is a fundamental precondition for individual autonomy. Second, the UNSC's competences also have the capacity to severely restrict collective autonomy by allowing the use of force or by issuing other sanctions against sovereign states. Therefore, the legitimacy of the UNSC requires (besides the effectiveness in pursuing its purpose) fulfilling procedural standards so as to minimise the danger that these far-reaching competences pose to autonomy. It should be noted that the discussed competences might require procedural standards that contradict one another.

Procedural standards of the UNSC's legitimacy

What legitimacy standards are implied by the range of the UNSC's competences discussed here? The Council has often been criticised, and reforms of both its membership structure and its procedures have been demanded. The first issue concerns in particular the veto of the permanent members.[6] Even though all members on the Council formally have one vote according to Article 27(1), the necessity to include 'the concurring votes of the permanent members' (Article 27(3)) gives them the power to block decisions. Besides the veto, further questions regarding the representativeness of the UNSC, in a world that is fundamentally different from the one of 1945, have been raised (e.g. Caron, 1993; Fassbender, 1998; Hassler, 2012). In this section, we first analyse the issue of the Council's membership structure. In a second step, we discuss how procedural standards regarding the decision-making process that go beyond the questions of membership may justify the three competences of the UNSC outlined above.

UNSC membership structure: delegation or participation?

Due to the restricted size and structure of permanent and elected members, the UNSC does not represent all UN Member States equally. Yet what kind of representation is required of this particular institution? We suggest that representation is important as it creates accountability as a mechanism to limit political power. Grant and Keohane define accountability as a process in which 'some actors have the right to hold other actors to a set of standards, to judge whether they have fulfilled their responsibilities in light of these standards, and to impose sanctions if they determine that these responsibilities have not been met' (2005, p. 26). Accountability, therefore, always includes elements of *ex post* control. Grant and Keohane further suggest distinguishing between *participation* and *delegation* models of accountability. Both models allow for various degrees of discretion versus *ex ante* instructions. However, they differ on the question of *who* is entitled to hold the powerful accountable: in the participation model, it is those affected, while in the delegation model, it is those entrusting them with powers. Representation can be understood in both ways as participation- or delegation-centred accountability. International institutions are often based on the delegation model. Therefore, what is at stake here is not a lack of accountability, but rather to whom those institutions are accountable – in the case of the delegation model, powerful states (cf. Grant & Keohane, 2005). From a normative perspective, the protection of autonomy through accountability standards is only possible if all subjected to the rules of an institution can hold it accountable.[7] Therefore, the participation model is the relevant legitimacy standard in order to guarantee meaningful accountability.

On the delegation model, the inequalities in the Security Council's membership structure are not incompatible with accountability. The Member States have delegated political power by consenting to an international treaty and to the corresponding procedures to check the authority holders. While this corresponds to the general standard of state consent in international relations, several normative problems connected with this understanding of accountability follow. First, the question of origin or source legitimacy arises – in particular for non-democratic states, but also for the international system providing sufficiently just background conditions (cf. Ronzoni, 2009) under which consent can be understood to be normatively binding (e.g. Buchanan, 2013; Christiano, 2010). Second, even though state consent can, to some degree, function as a protection for collective autonomy, it remains questionable whether these inequalities are compatible with autonomy. Third, in the case of the UN membership, the one-time consent of a state will bind all its future generations, even if the competences of the Security Council change.

Regarding the representativeness of the UNSC, the participation model – based on holding institutions accountable to those subjected to its rules – requires modifying the membership structure of the UNSC. Reform proposals concern mainly the enlargement of formal membership (permanent or non-permanent) and the improvement of representativeness (e.g. by more accurate regional distribution). As Hurd (2008) points out, these suggestions involve a trade-off between increasing the legitimacy of the UNSC for some, while reducing it for others. While this may be the case for the sociological legitimacy that individual Member States exhibit either as a belief in the UNSC's legitimacy or in terms of compliance, it is not true for the normative legitimacy of the Council. For example, an improved regional representation can increase the Council's legitimacy for all, not just those who 'benefit' from the representation. The UNSC's current structure is particularly problematic from the perspective of accountability to those subjected, since the Council's agenda mainly concerns developed countries while four of the five permanent members 'are from the Westernized, northern hemisphere, and even China's non-industrial status is rapidly changing' (Hassler, 2012, p. 93).

In conclusion, the participation model is normatively more robust than the delegation model because it is based on the all-subjected principle that seeks to promote the autonomy of all equally and not just one of the delegating states. It follows that the membership structure should be changed. Yet the argument of contributions has been used to justify the current structure of the UNSC. Historically, the veto was essential for bringing on board the states that could provide the necessary military power to realise the Council's purpose (Hassler, 2012, p. 35). Even if the international power structure has drastically changed since its foundation, the inclusion of the major powers is probably still the only way to bind them if compliance with the prohibition of use of force is the ultimate goal. This is a question of effectiveness and other feasible institutional alternatives. Since the participation of the powerful states is seen as necessary to maintain collective security, the UNSC's membership structure reproduces rather than overcomes the power inequalities of the states in the international system. This means that in the current setting, states' self-interest makes the UNSC a highly power-based forum.

The feasibility of changing the membership structure constitutes, therefore, a serious legitimacy challenge (e.g. Weiss, 2003). Keohane and Buchanan suggest the revisability of the terms of accountability as a legitimacy standard in itself. Based on the premise that there is reasonable disagreement about what accountability precisely entails, legitimacy cannot but depend on whether an institution facilitates 'principled, factually informed deliberation about the terms of accountability' (Buchanan & Keohane, 2006, p. 427). What does it mean that the terms of accountability must be revisable in light of critical reflection and discussion? For Buchanan and Keohane, this standard depends on feedback from external agents such as NGOs. In their own evaluation of the UNSC's legitimacy, Buchanan and Keohane (2011) evaluate the revisability of the UNSC's terms rather positively because its goals have been adapted. While we agree with this evaluation of the purpose, in our opinion this does not fully capture the revisability of the terms of accountability. Evaluating revisability should also concern the question of whether procedural standards are adaptable – particularly if the institutional competences change. In this respect, external actors' feedback is important and can be a good indicator of the need for change, although there will hardly be a unified view as to what about the terms needs to be adapted, and when. Therefore, we suggest that revising the terms of accountability should be considered one of the main standards for an international institution's legitimacy when its competences have changed. This form of revisability could also alleviate some of the problems of the delegation model (such as restricting the autonomy of future generations).

Now, how can the UNSC's terms of accountability be revised? Article 108 (or in theory 109) of the Charter determines the procedure through which the UN Charter can be amended. In short, amendments have to be adopted by a vote of two thirds of the members of the General Assembly and ratified by two thirds, including the permanent members. This means that the terms of accountability can be adapted; however, the requirements are highly demanding. Since the enlargement from six to ten elected members in 1965, no reform proposals have been successful. In 1993, the UN General Assembly passed a resolution to set up an Open-ended Working Group on Council reform.[8] However, it is questionable whether the UN, under the current rules for change and with the increased number of members, is still able to change the Council's membership structure. Therefore, the possibility to revise the terms of accountability poses one of the most pressing problems for the procedural legitimacy of the UNSC.

Assuming that the feasibility of changing the membership structure is not a given in the short- to medium-term, this changes the question to that of whether circumventing the UNSC could generate an alternative institution or whether its structural deficit drops the balance of reasons to the level of the non-institutional alternative. For these questions, the importance of the institution's purpose and its effectiveness in achieving this end are essential. Polarisation in the Security Council may increase to the point where non-institutional alternatives may be preferable. Yet, if stability considerations and the preservation of current international law matter, the transition costs resulting from abandoning the UNSC are significant. However, feasibility is not a static restraint; rather, it depends on the involved actors, timeframe, and practice (cf. Gilabert & Lawford-Smith, 2012, Erman and Kuyper this issue). Certain actions in the present may open up different options in the future. A particular problem in this regard arises if the institution itself contributes to keeping alternative institutions unfeasible. However, given that the purpose of the UNSC is of high importance, and assuming that a similarly efficient, alternative institution with a more appropriate membership structure is currently not feasible, the unequal membership structure of the Council is as such not a completely delegitimising feature. However, this does not mean that we should not try to change this structure or even seek to establish better alternatives. A more detailed discussion of feasibility and how the interplay of different actors in a multilevel system, such as states or citizens, is required to make these assessments for international institutions. This is of particular relevance, as the lack of political will on the part of certain powerful actors should not be taken to create binding obligations for others.

Alternatives to membership reforms: justifying the three competences of the UNSC

The different competences of the UNSC, the expanded reach of the UN membership, and the outlined deficits of the UNSC's membership structure point to the need for additional procedural standards to improve the balance of reasons of the UNSC's overall legitimacy. Two widely discussed procedural standards regarding the internal working methods of the Council are *transparency* and *deliberation*.

Transparency is crucial to achieve any form of accountability. Reliable information on how the institution is actually performing must be provided. However, under the conditions of incongruence between the subjected and the accountability holders, 'broad transparency' (Buchanan & Keohane, 2006, p. 426), making information accessible to agents external to the institution, is required. In terms of the UNSC's transparency, several aspects stand out. First, the UNSC's institutional link to the UN General Assembly should be considered: Article 24(3) states that 'the Security Council shall submit annual and, when necessary, special reports to the General Assembly for its consideration'. Second, the Council President regularly briefs non-members and the press about private meetings (Weiss, 2003, p. 154). Third, the accessibility for NGOs has been improved through informal exchanges, e.g. with the International Committee of the Red Cross (ICRC) or the NGO Working Group on the UNSC. Additionally, the so-called Security Council Report, a private but publicly funded independent organisation, aims explicitly at advancing the transparency of the UNSC.[9] While these structures do not fulfil the perfect ideal of broad transparency and need to be strengthened further, they are in our opinion sufficient to create the basis for legitimacy.

Discourse standards can increase the legitimacy of international institutions by enhancing both the quality and inclusiveness of the discussion (e.g. Johnstone, 2008; Steffek, 2003). From the start, the idea of the UNSC was to establish procedures that induce major military powers to consider one another's interests (Hassler, 2012, p. 31). In fact, the UNSC can also grant non-members access through Article 31: 'any Member of the United Nations which is not a member of the UNSC may participate, without vote, in the discussion of any question brought before the UNSC whenever the latter considers that the interests of that Member are specially affected'.[10] Furthermore, the number and scope of subsidiary bodies assisting the UNSC's functions have been continuously growing, and these serve to increase the Council's knowledge and transparency. In addition to country-specific bodies, the themes of terrorism and international tribunals, for instance, have several dedicated bodies.[11] Since the majority of bodies are chaired by non-permanent members and operate by consensus, they provide significant opportunities for UN Member States to get informed and have their say in discussions relevant to the UNSC's work. Furthermore, the UNSC sends missions of representatives to countries in crisis to hear the views of those affected (Weiss, 2003, p. 154).

We hold that the *decision-making competence* can be regarded as partly legitimised through standards of transparency, but the latter should be strengthened through discursive improvements, in particular via restrictions on the use of the veto. The draft resolution presented by the Small Five discusses possible restrictions on the veto and mentions: i) explaining the reason for using the veto; and ii) abstaining from the use of the veto in the 'event of genocide, crimes against humanity and serious violations of international humanitarian law'.[12] The requirement to make reasons public improves the discourse without preventing the abuse of the veto in the strict sense; it pressures the permanent members to use their power responsibly and in accordance with reasons that are acceptable to all UN members. Therefore, such discourse-theoretical improvements with regard to the use of the veto specifically are highly conducive to the UNSC's legitimacy and should be implemented in order to counter the inequalities embodied in the veto. Two other issues that deserve further attention, since they are areas of possible improvement, are the penholder system and the short term length of the elected members (Martin, 2018). However, the revisability of the terms of accountability remains problematic, even more so for the other two (newer) competences.

The *quasi-legislative competence* enables the Council to restrict the autonomy of its subjects even further, as it creates the capacity to interfere with their self-legislation. Therefore, more equal participation would be required to counterbalance the risks created by this competence. The existing deliberative standards are insufficient to effectively protect autonomy with regard to the quasi-legislative competence as they only provide access to the discussion in the Council to non-members when the UNSC itself grants it. Since neither the abolition of the veto nor the increase in membership seem realisable in the short- or medium-term, these competences should rather be exercised by the UN General Assembly.

Finally, the *referral competence* of the Council opens up questions of impartiality and independence as this competence may affect not only the legitimacy of the UNSC, but also that of the ICC by changing its jurisdictional reach. Since the purpose of a court requires impartiality and independence, the political nature of these referrals and the bias in case selection of the ICC,[13] to which the former contributes, leads to the de-legitimation of the ICC. In our view, this also creates a legitimacy problem for the UNSC. Consequently, the procedural standards required for this competence and the political nature of the Council are simply not compatible.

Conclusion

The aim of this paper has been to show how the concept of legitimacy can be applied to specific international institutions on using the example of the UNSC. By specifying the meta-coordination view of legitimacy based on the protection of the autonomy of those subject to the political power of an institution exercised through its rule-setting and applying competences, we have identified key aspects that are relevant for applying legitimacy to international institutions. In order to assess the risks and benefits that an institution creates for autonomy, i.e. the balance of content-independent reasons to comply, one needs to fully consider the purpose and the competences of an institution, as well as its efficiency, the feasibility of institutional alternatives, and procedural standards.

Applying the concept of legitimacy to the UNSC, therefore, requires determining its purpose and competence. We have shown that the UNSC's original mandate of maintaining peace and stability, with a focus on non-interference through the collective security system, has extended to the protection of human rights. Both purposes are not only minimally morally acceptable but crucial to individual and collective autonomy. We have determined three different competences of the UNSC – namely the decision-making competence, the quasi-legislative competence, and the referral competence. We have argued that the legitimacy assessment of the UNSC can be differentiated along these competences insofar as they require different procedural standards. On this basis, we have recommended that either extended competences should be reduced or the procedural standards should be improved. In particular, the competences of quasi-legislation and referral are rather problematic precisely because at present they are not sufficiently supported by procedural standards. Therefore, the broader purpose of the UNSC should be welcomed from the perspective of legitimacy, whereas its wider competences should be seen more critically.

Notes

1. We do not take a position on the conceptual question as to whether legitimacy should be understood as an exclusive 'right to rule' connected to a duty to obey. In particular, we do not discuss whether these reasons need to be pre-emptive, in the Razian sense, or 'weighty' in some other way (e.g. Raz, 1986; p. 46; Buchanan, 2010, pp. 83–84). As such, we refer to *sufficient*, content-independent reasons for compliance, which we consider to be compatible with both understandings.
2. What we consider here as not minimally morally acceptable is what falls beyond the scope of the right to do wrong in Adams' understanding (this issue).
3. For a more detailed account of how institutional competences influence the required legitimacy standards see Scherz (2019).
4. Voeten (2005) argues for a restricted version of this argument, namely that the legitimacy of the UNSC is given if it makes the unauthorised use of power costly, not impossible.
5. Buchanan and Keohane define minimal moral acceptability as the requirement to 'not persist in committing serious injustices' (2006, p. 419). Our definition highlights how these injustices can only be understood if equality is considered.
6. The Council consists of fifteen Member States: five permanent members and ten seats that are assigned by election for a set period of two years, as regulated in Article 23(2).
7. We apply the all-subjected not the all-affected principle in this paper (for a discussion of the difference between these principles, see Näsström (2011) and Scherz (2013).
8. A/RES/48/26 http://www.un.org/documents/ga/res/48/a48r026.htm .
9. Their report is accessible at http://www.securitycouncilreport.org.
10. Article 32 provides similar access for non-UN members.
11. Cf. https://www.un.org/sc/suborg/en/.
12. The S5 consisted of Costa Rica, Jordan, Liechtenstein, Singapore, and Switzerland. Their initiative lasted form March 2006 until May 2012, and later created the May 2013 launch of the follow-up project ACT for Accountability, Coherence, and Transparency by 22 governments. Draft resolution A/66/L.42/Rev.2, entitled 'Enhancing the accountability, transparency and effectiveness of the Security Council'.
13. See also Christiano's contribution in this issue on the legitimacy of the ICC's jurisdiction.

Acknowledgments

We are grateful to all the participants of the Justitia Amplificata workshop 'The Legitimacy of Global Governance Institutions' in Bad Homburg, January 2017, and of the panel 'International Law and Legitimacy' at the ECPR General Conference in Oslo, September 2017. In particular, we would like to thank Gleider Hernandez, Aiofe

O'Donogue, Knut Olav Skarsaune, Jens Steffek, Vegard Tørstad, and the anonymous reviewers for very thoughtful questions and comments. Funding was provided by Justitia Amplificata, Goethe University Frankfurt [grant number FOR 1206] and by PluriCourts, University of Oslo [grant number 223274].

Disclosure statement

No potential conflict of interest was reported by the authors.

ORCID

Antoinette Scherz http://orcid.org/0000-0002-6687-1525

References

Berdal, M. (2003). The UN Security Council: Ineffective but indispensable. *Survival, 45* (2), 7–30.
Besson, S. (2014). The legitimate authority of international human rights. In A. Føllesdal, J. K. Schaffer, & G. Ulfstein (Eds.), *The legitimacy of international human rights regimes. Legal, political and philosophical perspective* (pp. 32–83). Cambridge: Cambridge University Press.
Binder, M., & Heupel, M. (2015). The legitimacy of the UN Security Council: Evidence from recent general assembly debates. *International Studies Quarterly, 59*(2), 238–250.
Bodansky, D R. Wolfrum & V. Röben (Eds (Eds) (2008). The concept of legitimacy in international law. In R. Wolfrum & V. Röben (Eds (Eds) (Eds), *Legitimacy in international law (pp. pp. 309–317)*. Berlin: Heidelberg: Springer.
Bosco, D. (2014). Assessing the UN Security Council: A concert perspective. *Global Governance: A Review of Multilateralism and International Organizations, 20*(4), 545–561.

Buchanan, A. (2010). Legitimacy of international law. In S. Besson & J. Tasioulas (Eds.), *The philosophy of international law* (pp. 79–96). Oxford: Oxford University Press.

Buchanan, A. (2013). *The heart of human rights*. Oxford: Oxford University Press.

Buchanan, A. (2018). Institutional legitimacy. In D. Sobel, P. Vallentyne, & S. Wall (Eds.), *Oxford studies in political philosophy* (pp. 53–78). Oxford: Oxford University Press.

Buchanan, A., & Keohane, R. O. (2006). The legitimacy of global governance institutions. *Ethics & International Affairs, 20*(4), 405–437.

Buchanan, A., & Keohane, R. O. (2011). Precommitment regimes for intervention: Supplementing the Security Council. *Ethics & International Affairs, 25*(1), 41–63.

Caron, D. D. (1993). The legitimacy of the collective authority of the Security Council. *The American Journal of International Law, 87*(4), 552–588.

Christiano, T. (2010). Democratic legitimacy and international institutions. In S. Besson & J. Tasioulas (Eds.), *The philosophy of international law* (pp. 119–138). Oxford: Oxford University Press.

Christiano, T. (2012). The legitimacy of international institutions. In A. Marmor (Ed.), *The routledge companion to philosophy of law* (pp. 380–393). New York: Routledge.

Cronin, B., & Hurd, I. (2008). *The UN Security Council and the politics of international authority*. New York: Routledge.

Dahl, R. A. (1999). Can international organizations be democratic? A skeptic's view. In I. Shapiro & C. Hacker-Cordón (Eds.), *Democracy's edges* (pp. 19–36). Cambridge: Cambridge University Press.

Fassbender, B. (1998). *UN Security Council reform and the right of veto: A constitutional perspective*. Leiden: Martinus Nijhoff Publishers.

Forst, R. (2012). *The right to justification: Elements of a constructivist theory of justice*. New York: Columbia University Press.

Gilabert, P., & Lawford-Smith, H. (2012). Political feasibility: A conceptual exploration. *Political Studies, 60*(4), 809–825.

Grant, R., & Keohane, R. O. (2005). Accountability and abuses of power in world politics. *American Political Science Review, 99*(1), 29–43.

Habermas, J. (1996). *Between facts and norms: Contributions to a discourse theory of law and democracy*. Cambridge, MA: MIT Press.

Hassler, S. (2012). *Reforming the UN Security Council membership: The illusion of representativeness*. New York: Routledge.

Hurd, I. (1999). Legitimacy and authority in international politics. *International Organization, 53*(2), 379–408.

Hurd, I. (2008). Myths of membership: The politics of legitimation in UN Security Council reform. *Global Governance: A Review of Multilateralism and International Organizations, 14*(2), 199–217.

Johnstone, I. (2008). Legislation and adjudication in the UN Security Council: Bringing down the deliberative deficit. *The American Journal of International Law, 102*(2), 275–308.

Macdonald, T. (2016). Institutional facts and principles of global political legitimacy. *Journal of International Political Theory, 12*(2), 134–151.

Malone, D. (2004). Conclusion. In D. Malone (Ed.), *The UN Security Council: From the Cold War to the 21st century* (pp. 617–652). Boulder, CO: Lynne Rienner Publishers.

Martin, I. (2018, April 18). In hindsight: What's wrong with the Security Council? April 2018 monthly forecast [online]. *Security Council Report*. Retrieved from http://www.securitycouncilreport.org/monthly-forecast/2018-04/in_hindsight_whats_wrong_with_the_security_council.php

Näsström, S. (2011). The challenge of the all-affected principle. *Political Studies, 59*(1), 116–134.

Neusüss, P. (2008). *Legislative Massnahmen des UN-Sicherheitsrates im Kampf gegen den internationalen Terrorismus: Eine Untersuchung des Inhalts und der Rechtmässigkeit von Resolution 1373 unter besonderer Berücksichtigung der Reaktionen der Staaten*. München: Utz.

Raz, J. (1986). *The morality of freedom*. Oxford: Oxford University Press.

Rodley, N. (2015). Humanitarian intervention. In M. Weller, A. Solomou, & J. M. Rylatt (Eds.), *The Oxford handbook of the use of force in international law* (pp. 612–647). New York: Oxford University Press.

Ronzoni, M. (2009). The global order: A case of background injustice? A practice-dependent account. *Philosophy & Public Affairs, 37*(3), 229–256.

Sarooshi, D. (1999). *The united nations and the development of collective security: The delegation by the UN Security Council of its chapter VII powers*. Oxford: Clarendon Press.

Scherz, A. (2013). The legitimacy of the demos: Who should be included in the demos and on what grounds? *Living Reviews in Democracy, 4*, 1–14.

Scherz, A. (2019). *Tying the legitimacy of international institutions to their political power*. Manuscript submitted for publication.

Shraga, D. (2011). The Security Council and human rights – From discretion to promote obligation to protect. In B. Fassbender (Ed.), *Securing human rights? Achievements and challenges of the UN Security Council* (pp. 8–35). Oxford: Oxford University Press.

Steffek, J. (2003). The legitimation of international governance: A discourse approach. *European Journal of International Relations, 9*(2), 249–275.

Tasioulas, J. (2010). The legitimacy of international law. In S. Besson & J. Tasioulas (Eds.), *The philosophy of international law* (pp. 97–116). Oxford: Oxford University Press.

Tsagourias, N. (2011). Security council legislation, article 2 (7)of the UN charter, and the principle of subsidiarity. *Leiden Journal of International Law, 24*(3), 539–559.

Voeten, E. (2005). The political origins of the UN Security Council's ability to legitimize the use of force. *International Organization, 59*(3), 527–557.

Weiss, T. G. (2003). The illusion of UN Security Council reform. *The Washington Quarterly, 26*(4), 147–161.

Zysset, A. (2016). Refining the structure and revisiting the relevant jurisdiction of crimes against humanity. *Canadian Journal of Law & Jurisprudence, 29*(1), 245–265.

The legitimacy of occupation authority: beyond just war theory

Cord Schmelzle

ABSTRACT
So far, most of the philosophical literature on occupations has tried to assess the legitimacy of military rule in the aftermath of armed conflicts by exclusively employing the theoretical resources of just war theory. In this paper, I argue that this approach is mistaken. Occupations occur during or in the aftermath of wars but they are fundamentally a specific type of *rule over persons*. Thus, theories of political legitimacy should be at least as relevant as just war theory for the moral evaluation of occupations. This paper, therefore, draws on both traditions and argues that just war theory plays a limited role in identifying the purposes and appropriate agents of occupation authority, but that theories of legitimacy are necessary for explaining why and under which conditions foreign actors have the *right to rule* in the aftermath of armed conflicts.

Introduction

Much of the philosophical debate about legitimacy beyond the state has been focused on the legitimacy of international governance institutions such as the United Nations, the International Criminal Court, or the European Union (see the contributions by Scherz and Zysset, Christiano, and Erman and Kuyper, this issue). Only recently have political theorists begun to examine the exercise of *domestic* political authority by actors other than the nominally responsible state. One type of domestic non-state authority that gained significant political attention over the last decade is rule by occupying forces in the aftermath of armed conflicts. The public and political interest in these cases is no doubt due to the US-led military interventions in Afghanistan and, especially, Iraq. The subsequent occupations prompted various questions pertaining to the legitimacy of this kind of rule: Under what conditions, if any, are occupations justified? Which kinds of rights do legitimate occupiers hold vis-à-vis the occupied population? What is the legitimate scope and what are the justifying purposes of occupation authority?

To date, most of the philosophical literature on *jus post bellum* in general and occupations, in particular, has tried to answer these questions by exclusively employing the theoretical resources of just war theory (Lazar, 2012; Pattison, 2015).[1] In this paper, I argue that this approach is mistaken. Occupations occur during or in the aftermath of wars but they are fundamentally a specific type of *rule over persons*. Thus, theories of political legitimacy – that determine whether and under what conditions political authority is justified – should be at least as relevant as just war theory – which regulates the use of military force – for the moral assessment of occupations. This paper, therefore, draws on both traditions and argues that just war theory plays a limited role in identifying the purposes and appropriate agents of occupation authority, while theories of legitimacy are necessary for explaining why and under which conditions foreign actors have the *right to rule* in the aftermath of armed conflicts.

The article is organized into three sections. In the following section, I will briefly review the debate over occupation rule in the just war literature. This overview shows that there is no consensus concerning (a) the purposes, scope, and powers of occupation authority; (b) its legitimate agents; and (c) whether the answers to these questions depend on the justness of the preceding war. Next, I will sketch a general theory of institutional legitimacy in the following section. This theory is based on the idea that social institutions are *normative tools* that we create to pursue specific purposes. These purposes determine the scope and powers of legitimate institutions and the justificatory standards that apply to them. Subsequently, I will apply this theoretical framework to occupations. Here it will help me to answers the questions (a) through (c) for two types of occupations: *Fiduciary occupations*, that are restricted to the enforcement of pre-existing norms and *transformative occupations* that seek to change existing institutions.

The debate over occupation rule

It is possible to reconstruct the philosophical debate about the scope, purposes and appropriate agents of legitimate military rule as a critical response to the legal rules of humanitarian international law that regulate occupations (Jacob, 2014). These norms – formulated in The Hague Convention of 1907 and the Fourth Geneva Convention of 1949 – are organized around three principles: The *conservationist principle* regulates *what* legitimate occupiers may do (a); the *control principle* determines *who* exercises occupation authority (b); and the *principle of independence* asserts that the answers to both questions do not dependent on the justness of the preceding war (c).

The 'what' question

The conservationist principle states that occupiers must preserve the political, institutional, and legal *status quo* of the occupied state and understands occupiers accordingly as trustees that merely implement existing norms (Boon, 2009; Roberts, 2006). I will refer to this type of rule as *fiduciary authority*. The motive for this restrictive interpretation of occupation power is obvious: it is designed to prevent the acquisition of fully fledged political authority by means of war. There are at least three compelling reasons for wishing to prevent this: First, the protection of the political self-determination of the occupied people; second, the attempt to disincentivize war as a means of gaining political authority; and third, the belief that military success is an inadequate principle for assigning political powers and responsibilities.

While these arguments are intuitively convincing, the limited scope of fiduciary authority can be problematic as well. The conservationist principle has a tendency to preserve unjust and aggressive ante-bellum political structures. A crucial example for the limits of the principle are the occupations of Germany and Japan after World War II (Roberts, 2006). The Allies were convinced that a fundamental political transformation of the Axis states was necessary in order to reach a sustainable peace and to prevent them from committing future crimes against humanity.

These historical examples are cited by just war theorist today in order to argue for a less restrictive *jus post bellum* that allows for *transformative authority* to reform existing political institutions *if* this is necessary for achieving the just ends of the preceding war (Bass, 2004; Orend, 2000). Proponents of the conservationist principle caution against this reformist approach, arguing that a restrictive interpretation of occupation authority is more necessary than ever in order to tame neo-colonial interventions (Bain, 2003).

The 'by whom' question

The control principle states that whenever a foreign power has *de facto* military control over a territory it assumes some of the rights (i.e. to enforce existing laws and to levy taxes) and many of the duties (i.e. to uphold public order and to provide basic welfare) of the nominally responsible state (see Chehtman, 2015). While there is no realistic alternative to this arrangement *during* wars, this is not the case for occupations in the *aftermath* of armed conflicts. When the institutions of a defeated state cannot or should not resume their responsibilities, victorious belligerents can either assume these tasks themselves or transfer their control of the territory to a better-qualified actor (Fabre, 2016; Pattison, 2015). The establishment of the *United Nations Interim Administration Mission in Kosovo* after the NATO-led intervention is an example of such a decoupling of warfare and transitional administration. But victorious belligerents are by no means legally obligated to transfer their power to multilateral institutions. The UN-sanctioned American-British administration of Iraq is one recent example of the utilization of the control principle to legitimize occupations by former belligerents.

The rationales for the principle are, again, intuitively plausible. The control principle ensures, first, that the responsibility to govern falls on the only actor who has *at this moment* the capacity to do so. Secondly, the principle sets an epistemically unambiguous standard for assigning the obligation to govern to a specific actor: Whoever controls a territory, a fact that is rather easy to establish, assumes the responsibilities of the ousted government. Whereas the principle's first implication promises at least minimally *capable* occupiers, the second helps to identify the actors that have the *responsibility* to govern.

There are, however, some serious problems with the control principle as well. A first line of criticism asserts that, depending on the justness of the preceding war, the principle either produces an unfair distribution of responsibilities or an illegitimate distribution of authority. James Pattison (2015), for example, argues that the control principle tends to be *unfair* to just belligerents, since it imposes the burdens of governing on them for either practicing their right to self-defense or their willingness to protect others. Conversely, the control principle seems to produce *illegitimate* results, if it establishes the authority of a victorious but unjust belligerent, such as the Coalition in Iraq or the Russians in Crimea. Thus, the control principle potentially both disincentivizes the just use of force in assigning duties to successful belligerents and incentivizes the unjust use of force by adding political authority to the spoils of war.

A second problem with the control principle is that it is less reliable in assigning the responsibility to govern than its proponents had hoped. Belligerents who avoid military control of foreign territory, either by confining themselves to air strikes – with often disastrous results for the civilian population – or by quickly withdrawing their ground troops, can eschew the responsibilities of occupation. Both strategies for avoiding military control lead to the very responsibility gap that the control principle was designed to avoid.

The 'independence' question

The conservationist principle and the control principle are both manifestations of a third principle, the principle of independence. This principle purports that both the scope of occupation authority and the qualification of a belligerent for holding this kind of authority are independent of the causes and preceding stages of the war. The idea is that, in order to increase compliance, the legal rules of war should be as neutral, inflexible and objectively applicable as possible. As the previous sections have already implied, however, the problem with this line of thought is that inflexibility with respect to the causes of war and neutrality with respect to the belligerents' justness can lead to highly counterintuitive results. It would have prohibited the institutional transformation of Nazi Germany and it legalizes foreign rule after wars of aggression, Iraq and Crimea being recent examples. In what follows, I will attempt to demonstrate that these intuitive objections are well-founded and discuss in which ways the justness of the occupying party and the cause of war matter for an actor's legitimacy and the scope of its authority.

A theory of institutional legitimacy

One problem with the debate over the legitimacy of occupation authority is that it almost exclusively takes place within the framework of just war theory (Lazar, 2012). While the facts about the cause, proportionality and general justness of the preceding war are no doubt important for determining the proper scope and agents of post-war authority, they are hardly sufficient for this purpose: They neither provide a theory about the appropriate purposes and powers of political institutions, nor do they explain how actors gain and lose legitimacy, i.e. the right to exercise institutional powers. These types of question traditionally fall within the purview of theories of political legitimacy, which have yet not been applied systematically to occupation rule (an important exemption is Chehtman, 2015). This omission sets the task for the remainder of this paper. In this section I first sketch a general theory of institutional legitimacy which I will then apply to the assessment of occupations in the following section.

The purposes and powers of institutions

Institutions are indispensable building blocks of societies. They are systems of norms and practices that stabilize expectations, coordinate behavior and enable collective action towards specific institutional goals and purposes. Institutions accomplish these tasks by enabling and prohibiting certain actions, defining social roles, and assigning normative advantages and disadvantages to institutional agents. Examples of institutions include schools and universities, the criminal justice system, tennis clubs, and the political institutions of the state.

Drawing on work by John Searle (2010) I suggest to understand institutions as *normative tools*. According to this view, institutions are *tools* because we evaluate, justify and often design them in reference to specific purposes that they are supposed to fulfill. The criminal justice system, for example, is designed to determine, prevent, and punish criminal behavior. The powers of institutional roles within the system, such as the roles of judges, police officers, and lawyers, need to be justified in reference to these purposes and we evaluate criminal justice systems on the basis of how well they fulfill their assigned functions. Institutions are *normative* tools because they pursue their purposes not primarily through the physical or cognitive capacities of their agents but through altering the distribution of normative advantages and disadvantages. These advantages and disadvantages can be spelled out in Hohfeld (1919) terms: Institutions have a specific set of claim-rights, liberties, normative powers, and immunities as well as institutional duties and liabilities that enable and motivate them to coordinate the actions of their subjects and so to achieve their purposes. What distinguishes police officers from armed vigilantes, for example, are ultimately their rights (e.g. to use force and to issue directives), duties (e.g. to prevent criminal acts) and liabilities (e.g. being subject to political control), and not their training and equipment.

Before we turn to the question of institutional legitimacy, I want first to introduce a distinction between two categories of institutions; first-order and second-order institutions (Holm, 1995). These categories are defined by the type of purposes that a given institution fulfills and the corresponding normative advantages that it typically possesses. First-order institutions are restricted to applying, implementing, and enforcing norms, whereas second-order institutions have the power to set and to alter rules. The police, to give an obvious example, is a first-order institution that enforces rules that have been established by the legislature, a second-order institution. These different purposes affect the characteristic normative advantages and disadvantages of first- and second-order institutions: within their jurisdiction, second-order institutions usually have broad discretionary normative powers, i.e. the ability to set binding rules as they see fit. First-order institutions, in contrast, often lack discretionary rights. They are typically under a duty to exercise a limited set of liberty-rights and normative powers in accordance with pre-set instructions. With this distinction in hand we can now turn to the problem of institutional legitimacy.

Institutional legitimacy

Assertions about the moral standing of institutions can take one of two forms. Axiological statements about institutions assess whether and to what degree an institution embodies, promotes or realizes specific values such as justice or well-being. From a practical perspective, axiological judgements are obviously important for informing actions, but they do not, in and of themselves, prescribe or prohibit any course of action. By contrast, *normative* assessments are directly action-guiding. They refer to the rights, duties and normative powers of actors, i.e. what they can, may, should and must not do. In the philosophical debate on legitimacy, the concept typically indicates a *normative status* of institutions. A normative status is a status by virtue of which an actor or institution enjoys a certain set of rights and duties, powers and liabilities, that enable it to fulfill specific purposes (Searle, 2010; Taylor, 2015). It is defined 'by a pairing of a set of upstream entry conditions with a set of downstream consequences' (Taylor, 2015, p. 5). The status of being married, for example, is entered into by consenting to forming a legally recognized union with one's spouse and it has the consequence of creating special obligations of care and assistance between the parties.

What, then, are the entry conditions and consequences of institutional legitimacy? What are, in other words, the conditions that an institution needs to fulfill in order to count as legitimate and what rights and duties, powers and obligations arise from this status? Since institutional legitimacy is a much broader and more abstract status than, for instance, being married, the entry conditions and normative consequences are probably much more abstract as well. The question is then whether the characteristics of, e.g., legitimate schools, legitimate states, and legitimate military occupations have enough in common to establish a general concept of institutional legitimacy that can be applied to every type of institution. My strategy for addressing this question in the remainder of this section is to draw on the extensive literature on state legitimacy and to develop a more abstract definition of legitimacy that may be applied to a broad spectrum of institutions.

With regard to the *consequences* of legitimacy, there is wide agreement in the philosophical literature that legitimate states have the *right to rule* (e.g. Applbaum, 2010; Copp, 1999). However, this abstract consensus immediately breaks down when we compare the scope of this right – what activities fall under the right to rule – and the normative advantages that flow from it, in different theories of legitimacy. This contrast is instructive, since it derives from and refers to different views about the proper *purposes* of state institutions: Authors with libertarian leanings, for example, argue for a narrow conception of legitimacy that consists of the liberty-right to enforce natural rights and limited normative powers to arbitrate disputes over these rights (Nozick, 1974; Wellman, 1996). They see the state basically as a first-order institution with the purpose to enforce and apply, but not to create, binding rules. Neo-Kantians, on the other hand, see the state primarily as a second-order institution whose main function consists in *generating* binding norms under conditions of a reasonable pluralism (Christiano, 2004; Stilz, 2009; Waldron, 1999). This purpose, in turn, justifies a much broader conception of state authority that includes discretionary normative power to regulate most social interactions.

The important point here is not which side is right in this debate but that both employ the same methodology. The institution's purpose defines in both cases the legitimate scope of its activities and the normative advantages that it claims. Under both theories, scope and kind of authority are *purpose-dependent*.[2] The normative shape of a political institution is formed by its function just as the physical shape of a hammer is formed by its. Note that purposes play both a justifying and constraining role in this argument. They justify institutional normative advantages, but they also limit the scope of these advantages to cases that can be justified by the institution's purpose.[3]

The literature on state legitimacy does not only discuss the consequences of legitimacy but also the *entry or justification conditions*, i.e. the criteria a state must meet to be considered legitimate. There are, of course, dozens of theories of state legitimacy, but for our purposes, it is sufficient to distinguish between three groups of views. These theories are distinguished by the *deontic status* that they ascribe to state institutions and their purposes. They view the purposes of states as either morally (1) impermissible, (2) merely permissible, (3) or mandatory.[4]

The first theoretical perspective argues that an inherent impermissible purpose spoils the normative status of state institutions. Some theories of anarchism defend this position.[5] They contend that the key purpose of states, to exercise some kind of centralized authority, is always morally impermissible because it is supposedly irreconcilable with the fundamental value of human autonomy. For the anarchist this impermissible purpose suffices to render every conceivable state illegitimate, no matter how beneficial it might otherwise be. This reasoning can be extended to all types of institutions. If the purpose of the institution is impermissible, then it seems unjustified to grant it a normative status that enables it to pursue this purpose.

Consent theories are key examples of theories that view the establishment and support of authority structures as neither impermissible nor mandatory, but morally neutral (Locke, 1690; Simmons, 1979). According to this approach, we are neither under an obligation to create authority structures nor are we prohibited from doing so, given that we respect the rights of others in the process, which crucially includes their right not to be involuntarily subjected to political institutions. From this follows that the only way states can gain legitimacy is through the voluntary consent of the governed. This view rests on the intuitively convincing principle that autonomous persons can create normative liabilities for themselves by voluntarily accepting the authority of institutions. This principle, however, seems much better suited to explain the legitimacy of civil society organizations than that of large-scale political institutions which claim authority over entire societies (see Simmons, 2002).

A third branch of theories holds that political institutions are at least sometimes a *necessary* means to pursue morally mandatory purposes. Important examples of this approach are natural duty of justice theories.[6] They argue that we often need to coordinate our actions through institutions in order to discharge our independent – natural – moral duties not to harm or subject others (Kant, 1991; Stilz, 2009) or to rescue them from great peril (Wellman, 1996). In either case, it becomes morally mandatory, according to natural duty theorists, to 'support and comply with just institutions' and to 'further just arrangements not yet established' that help us to fulfill these duties (Rawls, 1971, p. 115). One important implication of this approach is that it suggests that the justification of morally mandatory institutions has an inherent instrumental dimension (Adams, this issue). Accordingly, whether a particular institution is legitimate depends, at least in part, upon how well it fulfills its purpose – a standard that is irrelevant for institutions legitimized through consent. What this exactly entails depends on the kind of purpose that the institution serves. The legitimacy of norm-setting second-order institutions usually depends on the fairness of their decision processes since there is typically widespread (reasonable) disagreement among the subjects about the value of different options. In cases in which all subjects have roughly equal stakes in the institution's decisions, this usually implies the need for democratic procedures. The legitimacy of first-order institutions, on the other hand, depends more directly on their capacity to effectively implement and enforce pre-existing norms and standards. Here too democratic procedures are preferable. They increase an institution's accountability and allow its subjects to overcome potential disagreement about its methods and priorities.

The relative merits of these theories are, again, less important than the similarities of their argumentative strategies. All three views consider the deontic status of the institution's purpose as the basis for determining whether an institution can achieve legitimacy, and, if so, through which *justificatory mode*. Institutions with impermissible purpose cannot become legitimate at all, institutions with merely permissible purposes depend on the consent of their subjects, and institutions with mandatory purposes can gain legitimacy vis-à-vis non-consenting subjects if they are reasonably just and effective.

If we accept the argument this far, institutional purposes determine on the one hand the scope and means of legitimate state authority and on the other hand the standards of justification that apply to it. I want to suggest that this pattern can be extended to institutional legitimacy in general. The purposes of institutions determine how they are to be justified, what they may do, and which means they may employ. To say that an institution is legitimate is, therefore, to say that it (1) is authorized by the relevant standards (2) to use necessary and proportionate means (3) to pursue its permissible purpose. The first part of this definition requires that legitimate institutions meet specific justificatory standards – consent, procedural fairness, or effective performance – that arise from their purposes. The second part stipulates that legitimate institutions may only employ the normative advantages – claim-rights, privileges, powers, and immunities – that are necessary and proportionate to their purposes. This condition ensures, on the one hand, that legitimate institutions have the normative advantages that they need to pursue their purposes at their disposal, but it also restricts them to the means that can be justified by these purposes. The third element stipulates that legitimate institutions may use their normative advantages only for tasks that are morally permissible and part of the institution's purview. This condition excludes morally impermissible purposes and prevents institutions and their leaders from corruptly co-opting an institution's powers for purposes that are in principle permissible but not part of the institution's mission. This understanding of institutional legitimacy implies that there are three different ways in which an institution can lack legitimacy. Either (1) the institution is not authorized to operate by the relevant standards, (2) its means are unnecessary or disproportional to its purposes, or (3) the purposes pursued by the institution are morally impermissible or fall outside of the institution's purview.

Occupation rule as a case of institutional legitimacy

In this section, I will now use this theory of institutional legitimacy to assess the legitimacy of occupation rule. More precisely, I will explore which purposes, if any, justify which kind of occupation authority and which agents – just belligerents, unjust belligerents or third parties – have the right to exercise this kind of power. I will investigate these questions separately for the two kinds of occupation authority that I have distinguished above – (a) fiduciary and (b) transformative occupations.

Fiduciary occupations

According to the proposed theory of institutional legitimacy, the normative advantages, modes of justification, and scope of activities of legitimate institutions depend on their purposes. In order to assess the legitimacy of fiduciary occupations, we need first to identify their purpose and explore then whether this purpose has the normative force to justify its powers and activities.

As I have already noted, the purpose of fiduciary occupations is to maintain public order and services during and in the immediate aftermath of armed conflicts. To this end fiduciaries are expected to act as trustees of the occupied. They merely apply and enforce the existing norms of the ousted state. My account of institutional legitimacy suggests that there are in principle two routes to legitimize this kind of rule. One must either show that the subjects of occupation authority have voluntarily consented to it or that it is impossible for them to discharge their natural moral duties without the help of fiduciary institutions. Let me consider both alternatives in turn.

The strength of consent theories is that they are intuitively plausible. The voluntary consent of autonomous persons to an institution's authority should be *sufficient* to justify its authority, or at least shift the burden of proof to the institution's critics. However, the question here is whether the consent of the governed is a *necessary* condition for the legitimacy of occupations. There is an epistemic and a categorical reason to doubt this. The epistemic reason is that it is nearly impossible to obtain meaningful and reliable expressions of consent during or in the immediate aftermath of wars. *Actual consent* in the form of voluntary promises or contracts between the occupiers and the occupied is difficult to obtain for obvious logistical reasons but also because the power imbalance between occupiers and occupied makes it hard to tell whether consent is given voluntarily and therefore valid. Moreover, possible indicators of *tacit consent* such as continued residence in the occupied territory, voting, or at least non-resistance (cf. Simmons, 2002) are compromised. They may be influenced by other factors such as ongoing conflict (continued residence), may not apply to the circumstances (voting), or may simply indicate resignation in the face of costly alternative behaviors (non-resistance).

A more categorical reason against consent as a necessary condition for the legitimacy of occupations is that the occupied might be under a moral duty to accept sufficiently just and effective occupations. This implies, of course, that the purposes of at least some instances of military rule are morally mandatory and that consent is therefore in these cases the wrong standard of justification. One way to make such an argument is to apply the idea of natural duties of justice to post-conflict situations.

Natural duty of justice theories have the immediate upside that they can explain the normative situation of the occupiers and occupied alike. Potential occupiers are, if natural duties of justice theories are correct, under a natural duty to establish and support just institutions, if these are necessary to protect the basic rights of the occupied (Rawls, 1971). Depending on the normative advantages of occupation institutions, the occupied are in turn under an obligation not to resist and to comply with these institutions, if this is necessary to discharge *their* independent moral duty to treat each other justly. So the justification of occupation rule towards a potential subject is *not* that it will benefit *her* but that she owes the benefit of just and effective political institutions to her neighbor – and vice versa (cf. Wellman, 1996).[7]

The question is now, what kind of duties may convey sufficient normativity into the process and how exactly is this normativity transmitted to political institutions? As I have already mentioned above there are variations of this argument that are based either on negative duties not to harm or to subject others or on positive duties to rescue them from grave peril. Both types of duties play an important role in explaining the normative dynamics in cases of occupations. Positive duties to rescue, on the one hand, explain the potential occupier's duty to uphold or to establish just and effective political institutions in post-conflict situations. The idea here is that we all have a limited duty to rescue others from grave danger and that living without effective political institutions that set, apply and enforce reasonably just laws is such a danger (Wellman, 1996). Negative duties not to harm and subject others, on the other hand, are well-suited to justify the occupiers' right to rule vis-à-vis the occupied. Natural duty of justice theories argue that this duty is impossible to fulfill in a state of nature without political institutions that publicly set, apply, and enforce rules. Their argument rests on the assumption that moral principles are open to a wide variety of reasonable interpretations. This indeterminacy makes it impossible even for well-meaning persons to treat each other justly without the help of institutions that set binding norms, settle disputes, and ensures that the law is equally and universally enforced.

It is now easy to see how this argument can be applied to the case of occupations. If the nominal responsible state loses control over part of its territory during a war, then the population of this territory finds itself in a position that at least partly resembles a state of nature scenario. Although the laws of the state are technically still valid, they will lose their coordination function without courts that apply them and law enforcement institutions that assure compliance. An instructive example of such a situation was Iraq's descent into chaos after the American invasion.

The American failure to make law enforcement an early priority of the occupation led to a vicious circle of violent crime, economic breakdown, more crime, and finally political disintegration and civil war (cf. Williams, 2009). The initial lack of effective policing and adjudication had two consequences. Criminal behavior became much less risky, whereas complex economic activities became much more so, since contracts and property rights were basically unenforceable. This led to an economic crisis, which gradually turned crime into the most lucrative industry. Extortion, robbery, and especially kidnapping became 'the best business in Baghdad' as a Shia man put it in an interview with the Guardian in 2007 (quoted in Hills, 2013, p. 95). Given these threats, the high availability of weapons, and the lack of alternatives, violence quickly became the normalized form of dispute resolution among Iraqis and the resulting revenge and honor killings further fueled a descent into anarchy (Green & Ward, 2009). Finally, the terrorized population turned to sectarian militias that offered protection in exchange for political and material support. These groups then used this support to engage in escalated criminal and political violence across ethnic lines that ultimately sparked the Iraqi civil war. Whereas this result is collectively irrational, it is the result of individually rational and morally at least excusable actions under conditions of insecurity.

The example of Iraq illustrates two features of post-conflict situations that are important for the justification of occupation rule. These situations are characterized by structural conditions that (a) force even well-meaning persons into harmful behavior and (b) are nearly impossible to overcome without third parties that assure general compliance. This triggers both a natural duty of potential occupiers to uphold the social order and a corresponding duty of the occupied to accept this authority as long as it is reasonably just and effective. I have argued in the last section that an institution's purpose determines the legitimate scope of its authority, the powers that it may exercise, and its mode of justification. What, then, follows from the purpose of upholding social order for fiduciary occupations?

The scope of fiduciary occupations is predetermined by the laws of the ousted state and conditional on its inability to exercise domestic authority. Fiduciaries only have the authority to implement and enforce existing laws – given that they are reasonably just – as long as the occupied state is incapable of doing so itself. Given their lack of democratic justification, fiduciary authorities should further focus on the provision of basic goods such as security, welfare, and conflict resolution and abstain from unnecessary interventions into the societies that they only temporarily administrate.

The purpose of temporarily upholding social order also shapes the powers of occupiers. It gives fiduciaries liberty-rights to enforce preexisting norms, claim-rights to non-interference, and non-discretionary normative powers to adjudicate conflicts. But it also ties the legitimate exercise of these advantages to this purpose, commits occupiers to norms of impartiality while exercising these powers, and withholds any legislative authority from them. Fiduciary occupations remain first-order institutions that may apply existing norms, but lack the authority to change them. This kind of purpose finally also defines their mode of justification. Fiduciary authority is instrumentally justified by how well it achieves its purpose to temporarily uphold social order during and in the immediate aftermath of armed conflicts. The mode of justification and the restricted scope of fiduciary authority imply that just and unjust belligerents are both in principle qualified and under an obligation to exercise this kind of rule. They are both potentially qualified since *de facto* authority, i.e. military control of a territory, is the necessary and sufficient condition for holding fiduciary authority (Chehtman, 2015). And they both have the right and duty to exercise fiduciary authority since the guarantee of basic social order and services is of such moral importance that less than ideal governance by unjust actors is, as a rule of thumb, often still preferable to no governance.

Nevertheless, even when they are on balance legitimate, fiduciary occupations are a normatively problematic form of foreign, undemocratic rule that subjects the occupied to unaccountable power and denies them influence over the methods by which they are governed. The scope of fiduciary occupations should, therefore, be as limited as possible and they should end as soon as minimally reliable domestic alternatives are available.

Transformative occupations

If the underlying norms of the occupied state are reasonably just, this restrictive interpretation of occupation authority makes good sense. By merely implementing pre-existing laws it respects the political self-determination of the occupied people and disincentivizes resorting to war for the sake of gaining discretionary legislative authority (Fox, 2012). The limited scope of fiduciary authority becomes problematic, however, if the implementation of the pre-war status quo would itself be inacceptable. In such cases, the *transformation*, not preservation, of the old social order seems morally necessary. Yet this purpose would grant occupying forces broad normative powers to establish new rules and institutions. Transformative occupations would therefore have a much wider authority than fiduciary ones. The question is then under what conditions, exactly, would any foreign actor have the right to transform the political institutions of another country? What purposes justify this kind of authority?

One answer that is frequently given in the *jus post bellum* debate is that transformative authority is justified only if it is necessary for the sustainable realization of the just causes of the preceding war (Bass, 2004; Orend, 2002). This may be referred to as the *cause dependence principle*. If a war has, for example, the just cause to protect an ethnic minority from genocide by state agents, then the victorious just belligerent has the right, and possibly the duty, to transform state institutions in such a way that the minority is protected from further violence for the foreseeable future. Conversely, the occupied population must accept these interventions if they are necessary to prevent future genocides. In this case, the fundamental rights of victims ground both the right to wage war and to exercise occupation authority. Whether there is a mandate for total transformation, as in the case of Germany after World War II, or more limited measures, like in Iraq in 1991, depends on what actions the war's just aims would necessitate.

This approach has three important advantages. First, it draws on a normative theory that explains the reasons for, scope of, and limits to transformative occupation rule. This is the theory of institutional legitimacy that I have sketched above. The cause dependence principle holds that transformative authority is only legitimate if it is necessary to realize the just ends of a just war. Accordingly, its scope and normative advantages need to be justified in reference to the war's purposes. These purposes, in turn, must deliver the normative basis to justify both the use of military force and occupation. Second, this way of thinking about occupation authority integrates questions of *jus ad bellum* and *jus post bellum* into a common framework which furthers our understanding of both principles. The claim is here that the actions necessary to realize the just causes of a war in its aftermath are an integral part of the actions that we need to consider when we justify war. This has two consequences. First, *ad bellum* legitimacy needs to include the right to transformative occupations if these are necessary to achieve the war's end. Second, if occupations are necessary to achieve a war's purpose, then their *expected* moral and material costs must be integrated into the proportionality tests of the *jus ad bellum* (Hurka, 2005). Third, the cause dependence principle avoids perverse incentives for going to war by limiting transformative authority to the realization of just causes of war.

I think, however, that the realization of just causes of war may be sufficient to justify transformative authority, but not necessary. I argue that the cause dependent principle applies the wrong normative standard to the right justificatory strategy. Let me explain. The argument rests on the idea that transformative authority is justified whenever it is necessary to ensure that its subjects will in future fulfill their fundamental duties that they have violated in the past. The problem is that the cause dependence principle restricts the relevant violations to cases that are severe enough to justify military force. This is so because, according to the principle, occupation authority may only help to achieve ends that already justified the preceding war. But this standard is too restrictive, because the *costs* of being the subject of foreign occupations are different than the costs of being the target of military force. An example might help to illustrate this point. Few theorists would argue that it is justified to wage a war in order to remove a misogynist regime that prohibits girls from getting primary education. The horrors of war, especially the unavoidable killing of innocent persons, are just too gruesome to justify a war for reasons other than collective self-defense, the prevention of a genocide, etc.. But whether or not a war would be justified in order to provide girls with access to education is the wrong standard for deciding whether or not transformative occupation would be justified to achieve this goal *if* a war had already been fought for other, stronger reasons. Establishing a transformative occupation under these circumstances or extending the scope of an independently justified fiduciary occupation, has clearly other – and lower – moral costs than waging war.

The obvious objection to this argument is that it is too permissive. This is problematic since being subject to undemocratic foreign rule is both inherently harmful and likely results in negative consequences as access to wide-ranging transformative authority incentivizes military aggression. Both points are well-taken but I think it possible to deflect much of their force if we take a closer look at the conditions that transformative authority has to fulfill in order to be legitimate. As I have argued above, institutions are legitimate if they (1) pursue permissible purposes, (2) utilize just and proportional means, and (3) are justified by the relevant standards to exercise their powers. These three criteria will help us now to restrict the purposes for which transformative authority can be utilized, the conditions under which it is proportional, and the actors that may exercise it.

(1) The first criterion is concerned with the purposes that are in principle capable of justifying involuntary institutions such as occupation rule. As we have seen above, only morally mandatory purposes can fulfill this condition. Involuntary institutions are only legitimate if they are necessary for fulfilling pre-existing moral duties. The problem is now that there is reasonable disagreement concerning what exactly we morally owe to each other. This is the reason, as I have argued above, for why we need legislative political institutions in the first place and it puts a burden of proof on transforming established institutions that usually reflect societal equilibria. I think, however, that there are two types of moral rights and corresponding duties that are important, unambiguous, and determined enough to justify the establishment of political institutions without the consent of the governed. These are, on the one hand, basic human rights such as the rights to life and security, sustenance, and basic liberties, and on the other hand the right to an infrastructure of just and effective political institutions that interpret, apply, and enforce these rights. Transformative occupations are therefore only justified if they are either necessary to protect basic human rights or to establish minimally fair and capable institutions.

(2) The second criterion assesses whether the means are proportional to the end. That is to say whether the *relevant* costs of transformative occupations are likely to outweigh their *relevant* benefits. This qualification is important since not all burdens and benefits of occupations influence their legitimacy. That successful occupations restrict the freedom of perpetrators to violate human rights, for example, does not count against them, whereas potential benefits that are not morally mandatory, such as economic growth, do not count in their favor. What, then, are the relevant burdens and benefits of transformative occupations? The relevant benefits are simply the realization of the morally mandatory aims of the institution. The relevant benefit of a transformative occupation with the purpose to protect an ethnic minority from violence is the degree to which it achieves this aim. But what are the relevant burdens?

The problematic aspects of transformative occupations derive from the fact that they are a form of foreign, undemocratic rule. Foreign, undemocratic authority structures are both intrinsically harmful and increase the probability of ineffective and abusive governance. They are intrinsically harmful in that they constitute a relational wrong; they violate the norm of equality both at the individual and the collective level. Undemocratic rule constitutes a *pro tanto* relational wrong at the individual level because it establishes a social hierarchy between rulers and the ruled that weighs the latter's opinions and interests as less worthy than the former's (see Viehoff, 2014). Foreign rule constitutes a *pro tanto* collective relational wrong because it establishes a social hierarchy between communities of rulers and ruled that implies that the latter are unable or unworthy to rule over themselves (cf. Ypi, 2013). Both arguments are powerful objections to occupation rule. The *pro tanto* wrongness of foreign and undemocratic rule shows that even legitimate occupations are harmful and that they should prioritize the expedient transition of power to a viable domestic (democratic) institution.

Besides these intrinsic problems, foreign, undemocratic rule also tends to produce bad results for the governed. This propensity is an important factor in calculating whether a transformative occupation's expected benefits outweigh its risks. The reasons for this tendency are epistemic, motivational, and capacity-based. Foreigners often do not fully understand the societies that they want to govern; they lack democratic control and other accountability mechanisms that force them to govern in the interest of the governed; and they usually have little empirical legitimacy which leaves them with bribery and coercion as their only means to initiate social cooperation (see Schmelzle & Stollenwerk, 2018). The combination of these factors all too often leads to policy solutions that are unsustainable once the occupiers leave. To remedy this problem occupiers should systematically include representatives of the occupied in their governance structures in order to better understand local interests and conflicts and attain at least a minimum of accountability and empirical legitimacy.[8]

The outcome of this discussion of the risks and harms of occupations is not that transformative authority is never justified but rather that it is a transitional, second-best option that can only succeed if the responsible actors have the right capacities and motivations. The last question that we have to address is whether certain groups of actors are categorically unqualified to exercise this kind of authority.

(3) I have argued above that unjust and just belligerents are both qualified and under an obligation to exercise fiduciary authority because *de facto* authority is sufficient for exercising fiduciary authority, the dangers of abuse are limited and it is hugely important that no authority vacuum emerges. The situation is different for transformative authority that seeks to create novel political institutions. Here, the danger of abuse is high and potential occupiers require not only de facto authority but also epistemic qualities, the right kind of motivations and the capacity to initiate social cooperation. I argue that this set of conditions typically rules unjust

belligerents out as potential occupiers and creates strong arguments for transferring transformative authority to international actors.

The idea that an aggressor might have the right to exercise transformative authority seems very odd from the outset, but it is surprisingly popular in the *jus post bellum* debate (see Feldman, 2004; Walzer, 2004). The example is here, again, the case of Iraq. The argument is, in a nutshell, Colin Powell's famous 'Pottery Barn rule': You break it, you own it. But what might be a good principle for determining liability in a china shop is a bad principle for transferring authority. The first reason is that actors, who have already waged an illegitimate war, have demonstrated either bad judgment or corrupt intentions that disqualify them from exercising far-reaching authority. The argument is here that the probability that they will rule badly or even abuse their power is simply too high, Iraq being a case in point. Moreover, it is likely that unjust aggressors are detested by the local population which makes successful governance unlikely and violent resistance probable. The second argument is that the Pottery Barn rule is relationally unjust. We cannot expect the *victims* of unjust belligerents to accept the authority of actors that have already demonstrated bad judgment or ill will towards them, no matter how qualified they might otherwise be. The third point concerns the incentives structure. If waging an unjust war would not disqualify a force from gaining transformative authority then this would create a powerful incentive to attack geo-strategically important or resource-rich countries that struggle with internal injustices capable of justifying institutional transformation but not a war. These three arguments make a strong case that the right to exercise transformative authority cannot be independent of the actors' *ad bellum* and *in bello* conduct.

Let me conclude with a final observation. While I have argued that just belligerents can in principle obtain limited transformative authority to pursue a handful of morally mandatory purposes if they observe strict standards of proportionality, the roles of belligerent and of ruler over the defeated party should nevertheless be separated whenever possible. Most of the arguments that speak against granting unjust belligerents transformative authority also apply, to a lesser degree, to just belligerents. Whoever fought a bloody war will not be able to draw on the goodwill of the local population. And feelings of revenge and fears of retribution may influence the way in which combatants rule. I, therefore, agree with James Pattison (2015) that the responsibility to exercise post-conflict authority should ideally be assigned to specialized international organizations or multilateral coalitions. This might not be possible for fiduciary occupations during wars, but it should be possible for transformative occupations. Moreover, separating the adversarial role of combatants from the governing role of occupiers not only seems more likely to produce good results but also fairer for just belligerents. There is no reason why the ones who have already sacrificed life and limb should also pay the tab for building sustainable, peaceful institutions.

Conclusion

I have argued for the thesis that theories of institutional legitimacy, and not just war theory, are foundational for understanding the conditions under which occupation rule is legitimate. The approach to institutional legitimacy that I introduce in this paper is built around the idea that an institution's purpose determines the legitimate scope of its activities, its normative advantages, and the relevant standards of justification. Applied to questions of occupation rule, this approach helps us to differentiate between two kinds of occupation authority – fiduciary and transformative occupations – that pursue different purposes, justify different powers, and demand different qualities of potential occupiers. But this shift of focus from just war theory to theories of legitimacy does not render facts about the cause, proportionality and general justness of the preceding war obsolete for the legitimacy of occupations. The cause of war is still a consideration in justifying purposes of transformative occupations, and the *ad bellum* and *in bello* justness of the belligerents determines whether they are at least in principle qualified to exercise transformative authority. But not only do theories of legitimacy need to consider the facts of war, just war theory needs conversely to contemplate the risks and inevitable relational wrongs that occupations entail. Even legitimate occupations have significant moral costs that we need to be cognizant of when we weigh the proportionality of war.

Notes

1. Important early contributions to the wider debate about the *jus post bellum* include Orend (2000, 2002), Bass (2004), Bellamy (2008), and Recchia (2009). Recent work by Walzer (2004), Mcmahan (2009), Bazargan (2013), and Chehtman (2015) has a narrower focus on the legitimacy of occupations.
2. For a similar argument see Rossi (2012).
3. This point is made by Locke in §139 of the Second Treatise (1690).
4. This distinction was developed by Nate Adams (). For a similar distinction between morally optional and non-optional institutional purposes see Schmelzle (2015, p. 142).
5. See Wolff (1970).
6. Another prominent example is Joseph Raz' service conception of authority (1986).
7. Mcmahan (2009, p. 104) comes close to making this argument when he claims that occupations are justified to those that benefit from them because their consent can be presumed.
8. See Chopra and Hohe (2004) and Recchia (2009) for concrete suggestions how an increased participation of local communities could be accomplished.

Acknowledgments

I would like to thank Andreas Cassee, Amy Thompson, Juri Viehoff and two anonymous reviewers for CRISPP for extremely helpful questions and comments.

Disclosure statement

No potential conflict of interest was reported by the author.

Funding

This work was supported by the German Research Foundation (DFG) within the Collaborative Research Center "Governance in Areas of Limited Statehood" [SFB 700] at Freie Universität Berlin.

References

Adams, N. P. (this issue). Institutional legitimacy. *Journal of Political Philosophy, 26*, 84–102
Applbaum, A. I. (2010). Legitimacy without the duty to obey. *Philosophy & Public Affairs, 38*, 215–239.
Bain, W. (2003). *Between anarchy and society: Trusteeship and the obligations of power*. Oxford: Oxford University Press.
Bass, G. J. (2004). Jus post bellum. *Philosophy & Public Affairs, 32*, 384–412.
Bazargan, S. (2013). Proportionality, territorial occupation, and enabled terrorism. *Law and Philosophy, 32*, 1–23.
Bellamy, A. J. (2008). The responsibilities of victory: Jus post bellum and the just war. *Review of International Studies, 34*, 601–625.
Boon, K. (2009). Obligations of the new occupier: The contours of a jus post bellum. *Loyola of Los Angeles International and Comparative Law Review, 31*, 101–128.
Chehtman, A. (2015). Occupation courts, *jus ad bellum* considerations, and non-state actors: Revisiting the ethics of military occupation. *Legal Theory, 21*, 18–46.
Chopra, J., & Hohe, T. (2004). Participatory intervention. *Global Governance, 10*, 289–305.
Christiano, T. (2004). The authority of democracy. *The Journal of Political Philosophy, 12*, 266–290.
Copp, D. (1999). The idea of a legitimate state. *Philosophy & Public Affairs, 28*, 3–45.
Fabre, C. (2016). *Cosmopolitan peace*. Oxford: Oxford University Press.

Feldman, N. (2004). *What we owe Iraq: War and the ethics of nation building*. Princeton: Princeton University Press.
Fox, G. H. (2012). Transformative occupation and the unilateralist impulse. *International Review of the Red Cross, 94*, 237–266.
Green, P., & Ward, T. (2009). The transformation of violence in Iraq. *The British Journal of Criminology, 49*, 609–627.
Hills, A. (2013). *Policing post-conflict cities*. London: Zed Books.
Hohfeld, W. N. (1919). *Fundamental legal conceptions. As applied in judicial reasoning*. New Haven: Yale University Press.
Holm, P. (1995). The dynamics of institutionalization: Transformation processes in Norwegian fisheries. *Administrative Science Quarterly, 40*, 398–422.
Hurka, T. (2005). Proportionality in the morality of war. *Philosophy & Public Affairs, 33*, 34–66.
Jacob, D. (2014). *Justice and foreign rule: On international transitional administration*. Basingstoke: Palgrave.
Kant, I. (1991). *Kant: Political writings*. Cambridge: Cambridge University Press.
Lazar, S. (2012). Scepticism about jus post bellum. In L. May & A. Forcehimes (Eds.), *Morality, jus post bellum, and international law* (pp. 204–222). Cambridge: Cambridge University Press.
Locke, J. (1690). *Second treatise of government and a letter concerning toleration*. Oxford: Oxford University Press [2016].
Mcmahan, J. (2009). The morality of military occupation. *Loyola of Los Angeles International and Comparative Law Review, 31*, 7–29.
Nozick, R. (1974). *Anarchy, state, and utopia*. New York: Basic Books.
Orend, B. (2000). Jus post bellum. *Journal of Social Philosophy, 31*, 117–137.
Orend, B. (2002). Justice after war. *Ethics & International Affairs, 16*, 43–56.
Pattison, J. (2015). Jus post bellum and the responsibility to rebuild. *British Journal of Political Science, 45*, 635–661.
Rawls, J. (1971). *A theory of justice* (Revised ed.). Cambridge: Harvard University Press.
Raz, J. (1986). *The morality of freedom*. Oxford: Clarendon Press.
Recchia, S. (2009). Just and unjust postwar reconstruction: How much external interference can be justified? *Ethics & International Affairs, 23*, 165–187.
Roberts, A. (2006). Transformative military occupation: Applying the laws of war and human rights. *American Journal of International Law, 100*, 580–622.
Rossi, E. (2012). Justice, legitimacy and (normative) authority for political realists. *Critical Review of International Social and Political Philosophy, 15*, 149–164.
Schmelzle, C. (2015). *Politische Legitimität und zerfallene Staatlichkeit*. Frankfurt: Campus.
Schmelzle, C, & Stollenwerk, E. (2018). Virtuous or vicious circle? governance effectiveness and legitimacy in areas of limited statehood. *Journal Of Intervention and Statebuilding, 12*, 449–467.
Searle, J. R. (2010). *Making the social world: The structure of human civilization*. Oxford: Oxford University Press.
Simmons, A. J. (1979). *Moral principles and political obligations*. Princeton: Princeton University Press.
Simmons, A. J. (2002). Political obligation and authority. In R. Simon (Ed.), *The Blackwell guide to social and political philosophy* (pp. 17–37). Malden: Blackwell.
Stilz, A. (2009). *Liberal loyalty. Freedom, obligation, and the state*. Princeton: Princeton University Press.
Taylor, K. A. (2015). How to Hume a Hegel-Kant: A program for naturalizing normative consciousness. *Philosophical Issues, 25*, 1–40.

Viehoff, D. (2014). Democratic equality and political authority. *Philosophy & Public Affairs, 42,* 337–375.
Waldron, J. (1999). *Law and disagreement.* Oxford: Oxford University Press.
Walzer, M. (2004). Just and unjust occupations. *Dissent, 51,* 61–63.
Wellman, C. H. (1996). Liberalism, samaritanism, and political legitimacy. *Philosophy & Public Affairs, 25,* 211–237.
Williams, P. (2009). *Criminals, militias, and insurgents: Organized crime in Iraq.* Carlisle: Strategic Studies Institute.
Wolff, R. P. (1970). *In defense of anarchism.* Berkeley: University of California Press.
Ypi, L. (2013). What's wrong with colonialism. *Philosophy & Public Affairs, 41,* 158–191.

Index

accountability 9, 53, 67, 92, 96, 102–106, 128
actors 3, 7, 46, 64, 85, 102, 105, 112, 115, 117–118, 127–129
all-affected principle 39–42
applied principle 38–40, 42
arbitrary power 17, 53–54, 58, 64
armed conflicts 112–114, 121, 124

belligerents 115–116, 121, 125, 128–130
Bodansky, D. R. 96
Bosco, D. 98, 100
Buchanan, A. 96, 104

cause dependence principle 125–126
charter 24, 53, 61–62, 67–68, 77–78, 97, 99–101, 104
Christiano, Thomas 45, 96
circumscribed jurisdiction 82–84
civil society 43–47; actors 44–46
coercive power 75
Cohen, G. A. 42
collective autonomy 93–96, 99, 101, 103, 107
competences 92, 95–96, 99–108
conceivable state illegitimate 119
conservationist principle 113–115
constitutionalization 9, 68
content-independent reasons 74, 92–93, 107
control principle 113–115
cooperation 8, 15–16, 79–80
Crawford, James 68
crimes 68, 72–79, 81–82, 84–86, 106, 114, 123
criminal justice systems 116–117

defective legitimacy 83
delegation model 102–104
deontic status 5, 17

domestic institutions 4, 7–8, 96
domestic law 7–9, 60–61, 63, 65

effective political institutions 122–123, 127
empirical legitimacy 128
equality 8, 55–56, 58–63, 67, 73, 79, 82–83, 85, 127
extant purpose 13, 24–27

feasibility 3, 6–7, 31–35, 37, 39–41, 43–45, 47, 87, 92, 95, 97, 103–105; claims 32–33; considerations 33, 35, 37–40, 47; constraints 3–4, 7, 31–32, 34, 36–39, 42–43, 46–47, 62; framework 32, 34, 39, 43, 46–47; role of 32, 34, 39
feasible institutional alternatives 20–21, 95, 103
fiduciary authority 114, 124–125, 128
fiduciary occupations 113, 121, 124, 129
first-order institutions 117–118, 120, 124
fitness constraint 32, 34, 37–38, 41–42
functional constraint 32, 34–38, 40–42

global democracy 31–36, 38–39, 41–43, 47; debate on 31–32, 34, 36
Grant, R. 102

Hohfeld, W. N. 117
Hurd, I. 103

impartiality 76, 107, 124
individual autonomy 3, 5, 27, 65–67, 94, 101
individual rights 46, 53, 55–56, 58–59
injustices 82–83
institutional agents 83, 116
institutional legitimacy 3–5, 12–13, 17, 113, 116–118, 120–121, 125, 130; general theory of 4, 113, 116
institutional powers 8, 116

institution illegitimate 14, 18, 20, 22
institution's legitimacy 16–17, 21
international community 7, 75, 77–80, 85–86
International Criminal Court (ICC) 7, 61–62, 67, 72–76, 78–88, 101, 107, 112
international criminal justice system 73, 78–80, 82
international law 2, 4, 6–9, 44–46, 52–55, 59–69, 73, 77, 80, 92, 99–100
international rule of law 3, 5, 52–55, 59–60, 62–65, 67–69; institutional contours of 67; purpose of 64

jurisdiction 3, 8, 68, 72–73, 75–77, 79, 81–82, 84–85, 87–88, 117; arbitrary circumscription of 75; state consent and 79
justice theories 119, 122–123
justification 2, 5, 19, 37–40, 53, 77, 82, 86, 94, 96, 120–122, 124, 130

Keohane, R. O. 96, 102, 104

legal jurisdiction 75–76, 82
legitimacy discourses 2, 5, 7–9, 27
legitimate institutions 5, 9, 113, 120–121
legitimate occupations 128, 130

medical institution 20–22
military force 99–100, 113, 125–126
mode of justification 121, 124
moral justification 76–77, 82
moral power 74–75, 82

Nardin, Terry 61
non-state actors 8, 44, 46, 74, 76
normative political principles 32, 34–35, 39–40, 42
normative political theory 32, 34, 47
normative principles 3, 31–32, 36, 47

occupation authority 112–116, 121, 125–126, 130; legitimacy of 112, 116
occupations 112–116, 122–123, 125–128, 130

participation model 92, 102–103
Pattison, James 115, 129
peace 5, 25, 61, 97–100
policy processes 43–46
political legitimacy 2, 31, 47, 81, 113, 116; theories of 113, 116
political society 74–75, 77

political theory 32, 34, 47
principle-kind aspect 35, 41
principle of democracy 35, 38
principle of justice 35, 38
procedural standards 92–93, 96–97, 101–102, 104–105, 107–108
purpose-dependent theory 4

quasi-legislative competence 92, 100, 106–107

referral competence 92, 101, 107
Rome Statute 62, 72–74, 78, 80–82
Rome Treaty 101
rule of law 3, 52, 54–60, 62–63, 65, 67, 73, 83, 87; *see also* international rule of law
Rule of Law Index 57

Searle, John 116
second-order institutions 117–118, 120
Security Council 3, 5, 53, 61, 64–65, 72–73, 77–78, 80–81, 84, 91, 94, 96, 104–105
Shraga, D. 99
state actors 76
state authority 2, 101, 118
state autonomy 54, 63–67, 101
state institutions 118–119
state legitimacy 2–4, 9, 12–14, 17, 22, 118–119
state of affairs 22, 33–34, 37
state power 55, 61, 65, 68
state sovereignty 3, 5, 68–69
subjects of international law 64, 66–68

Tomuschat, Christian 68
transformative authority 114, 125–130
transformative occupations 113, 121, 125–130
transparency 96, 105–106

United Nations Security Council (UNSC) 91–92, 97–108; changing competences of 99; membership structure 102; procedural standards of 101
United States 20, 25–26, 72, 78–79, 81, 86–88, 98

voluntary institutions 16

war 78, 113–116, 122–123, 125–126, 129–130
war crimes 72, 74, 77–78, 84
war theory 112–113, 116, 130